contents

Vincent Ryan OSB

THE SHAPING OF SUNDAY

Sunday and Eucharist in the Irish Tradition

VERITAS

First published 1997 by
Veritas Publications
7-8 Lower Abbey Street
Dublin 1

Copyright © Vincent Ryan OSB 1997

ISBN 1 85390 352 3

British Library Cataloguing
in Publication Data.
A catalogue record for
this book is available
from the British Library.

Cover illustration: *Walking to Mass,* painting by J.H. Craig,
reproduced by kind permission of the Crawford Art Gallery, Cork
Cover design by Bill Bolger
Printed in Ireland by Betaprint Ltd, Dublin

For Íde
and the memory of our parents

introduction

It was a bright autumn morning as the papal helicopter hovered over Dublin's Phoenix Park. There an immense throng of eager, expectant people was gathered for the occasion. Pope John Paul II had arrived to celebrate his first public Mass on Irish soil. It was 29 September 1979.

For those who were present, or even watched it on television, the experience is indelibly etched on the memory. It was an extraordinary manifestation of Catholic faith and eucharistic devotion. For some older folk who watched the Mass, it recalled the Eucharistic Congress of 1932.

It is good to recall an important point made by the Pope in the course of his homily. This related to Irish people's fidelity to the Mass, especially the Sunday Mass. It was an appeal to remain always faithful to this tradition. Here are his words:

> On Sunday mornings in Ireland, no one seeing the great crowds making their way to and from Mass could have any doubt about Ireland's devotion to the Mass. For them a whole Catholic people is seen to be faithful to the Lord's command: 'Do this in memory of me.' May the Irish Sunday continue to be the day when the whole people of God – the 'pobal Dé' – makes its way to the house of God, which the Irish people call the house of the people – 'Teach an Phobail.' (*The Pope in Ireland*, Veritas, 1979, p. 11)

When we survey the road travelled since the papal visit, it

is clear that profound changes have taken place both in the secular and religious spheres. We Irish are still a Mass-going people and the majority are practising Catholics. But successive statistics register a downward trend. Significant numbers of people, especially among the younger age groups and those in urban areas, are opting out of Sunday Mass and are rarely seen inside a church. Also significant and worrying is the diminishing number of candidates to the religious and clerical life.

We are witnessing the erosion of Sunday as a sacred day, a eucharistic day, a day of prayer, of rest, of family. Disappearing before our eyes is a 'culture of Sunday', a culture associated with going to Mass, wearing one's 'Sunday best', abstaining from 'servile work', a day of social and family obligations when it was expected that the whole family would be gathered for the special Sunday lunch. So much of that social, cultural side of Sunday has changed in recent years. People have become more individualistic, the young prefer to do their 'own thing'. Sunday trading, in spite of strong resistance from Church leaders, has become increasingly the norm. Sunday, like other religious institutions, is being gradually secularised; for an increasing number of people it is simply the second day of a leisure weekend or it is a working day like any other.

But if there are problems there are also opportunities. My intention is to be positive and constructive. We cannot turn the social tide back, but we can help create a future out of the riches of our tradition and the resources of the present. The faith is still strong, and Irish people are still in general a people of religious feeling – 'cine cráibhtheach' – as Douglas Hyde described us.

As we plan our future, it is good to return to the sources of Irish spirituality. This book is all about traditional Irish devotion to the Sunday and the Eucharist, these inseparable realities which make up the Lord's Day. From our study of history and the sources, both written and oral, there emerges an inspiring vision of the Sunday celebration. Not a complete vision, since we need to enlarge our mental horizons to include other traditions; and we must also take account of contemporary theology and Church teaching. But our own native tradition is an indispensable source to be studied and availed of. It is not a treasure to remain buried.

My own interest in this subject was aroused over thirty years ago when asked to give a talk titled 'Every Sunday an Easter Sunday' at the Glenstal Liturgical Congress of Easter 1964. In preparation for that lecture I availed of the generous scholarship of an tAthair Diarmuid Ó Laoghaire SJ, who placed at my disposal a selection of those beautiful Irish Sunday prayers which are Gaelic Ireland's most original contribution to a spirituality of Sunday. The title of my book, *Welcome to Sunday* (Veritas, 1980), was suggested by these prayers which welcome Sunday as a day of joy and celebration, and welcome Christ as the 'King of Sunday', 'Rí an Domhnaigh'.

In spite of the great number of footnotes this is a pastoral rather than a scholarly work, although I have referred throughout to the sources and to specialist studies. The notes may be of use to the student who wishes to explore this subject more fully, but for the average reader they can be safely ignored. My principal aim is to share a vision of the Irish Sunday, past and present, to bring encouragement to pastors and people by making them better informed about their rich spiritual heritage; and so to contribute in some small way towards a richer experience of Sunday as 'the day which the Lord has made'.

I gratefully acknowledge help received in the writing of this book. In my own community I have been aided in a scholarly way by Fr Placid Murray and Fr Gerard MacGinty (medieval Latin) as well as by Br Colmán Ó Clabaigh (medieval Irish history). Fr Ambrose helped me in a very practical way with the word-processing. To those outside the community my special thanks go to Fr Diarmuid Ó Laoghaire who read the chapter 'Sunday Prayers of the People' and made very helpful suggestions. Finally, I wish to express my appreciation and thanks to Fr Brian Magee CM who read the manuscript with a view to publication, and also to Fiona Biggs, Managing Editor of Veritas Publications, for her patience and encouragement.

Vincent Ryan OSB
9 June 1997
Feast of St Colum Cille

1
the shaping of sunday

The Gaelic word for Sunday tells us something about the day itself. It takes two forms: 'An Domhnach' and 'Dia Domhnaigh', both signifying 'the Lord's Day'. These terms correspond to the Latin *Dominica* or *Dominica dies.* Sunday is the 'dominical day', the day on which Christ, by rising from the dead, manifested himself as Lord (*Kyrios*). No name is more significant or richer in associations than that of 'the Lord's Day'. In the Roman Church it has always been the official name for the weekly day of worship and rest. It is fortunate that the Irish Church adopted this form of name in preference to 'Sunday' with its pagan associations.[1]

It is interesting to learn that the word 'Domhnach' could also designate a church building. It is claimed that there are nearly forty townlands in Ireland whose names are formed by, or begin with, 'Donagh', which is the anglicised form of 'Domhnach'. Thus we have Dunshaughlin ('Domhnach-Sechnaill'), the Church of Sechnall. St Sechnall, or Secundinus, is reputed to have been a nephew of St Patrick. It was believed that all the churches that bear the name of Domhnach were founded by St Patrick and were called so because he marked out their foundation on a Sunday.[2]

Christian Latin provides a similar association of words. In North Africa and Rome, in the third and fourth centuries, the word *Dominicum* designated both the Eucharist and the church building. In his history of the Roman Mass, J.A. Jungmann observes: 'This formation of a name which calls the Mass the celebration of Christ is parallel to that which calls Sunday the day of Christ (*Dominica*) and the Christian place of worship the house of Christ, the house of the *Kyrios* (*kyriakon* = church).'[3] Language and tradition thus bear witness to the intimate connection between 'the Lord's Supper', 'the Lord's Day', and 'the Lord's House'.

From Sabbath to Sunday

In the earliest period of the Irish Church, Saturday too was venerated as a sacred day. The reason for this lies in the fact that it corresponds to the biblical Sabbath, and its observance is prescribed by the Decalogue. As such it could be said to be of divine institution. Jesus, who claimed to be 'master even of the Sabbath', observed this sacred day and never abrogated the commandment to worship on it.[4] For the Church, however, this day has been superseded by the day following the Sabbath, the day consecrated by the Resurrection, the Day of the Lord.

Celtic Christianity was not alone in honouring Saturday as the Sabbath and making it a day of prayer and worship. Sabbath observance is witnessed to in both East and West in the early centuries of the Church. Willy Rordorf has traced this development in his important work, *Sunday*: 'From the time of Hippolytus onwards, particularly in the fourth century, there is an increasing amount of evidence for the Christians' practice of worshipping on the Sabbath.'[5] This worship often included the celebration of the Eucharist (normally not celebrated on weekdays). St Augustine testifies to this in North Africa. Before him Tertullian had noted how Christians did not kneel or fast on Saturday.

The monks of Egypt observed Saturday as a sacred day. We learn from Palladius (c.365-c.425) that the monks of Nitria occupied the church only on Saturday and Sunday, during which they celebrated the Eucharist. The celebration of Saturday and Sunday was common throughout Egypt and the East at this time.[6]

The Celtic practice of observing the Sabbath may derive indirectly from Egyptian monasticism via Lérins which had links with this source and where, according to tradition, St Patrick studied. The Irish Church began at a time when

Sabbath worship was strong in parts of Christendom. This practice took root in the Celtic Church of Ireland and Britain, and lasted longer in these countries than elsewhere. With the disapproval of the Roman Church, Sabbath worship disappeared rather rapidly outside these islands after the fifth century.[7]

There is evidence that on the island of Iona, off the west coast of Scotland, where St Colum Cille founded his great monastery and centre of evangelisation, Saturday was observed as a sacred day, a day of rest and blessing. It was even called the Sabbath and was honoured as such. In Adomnán's Life of St Columba there is a beautiful passage in which the saint speaks of his imminent death. This occurs at the beginning of the midnight office for Sunday 9 June 597. From this passage we see how both these days, the Sabbath (Saturday) and the Lord's Day (Sunday) were venerated:

> The venerable man made a statement to this effect: 'This day is called in the sacred books *Sabbath*, which is interpreted rest. And truly this day is for me a Sabbath, because it is my last day of this laborious life. In it after my toilsome labours I keep Sabbath; and at midnight of this following venerated Lord's day, in the language of the Scriptures, I shall go the way of the Fathers. For now my Lord Jesus Christ deigns to invite me. To him I shall depart, I say, when he invites me, in the middle of the night.[8]

From about the time of St Colum Cille there is a decline of Saturday observance and a growing veneration of Sunday. This process is attributed to Romanising influences at work between 600 and 800. In England Theodore of Tarsus, Archbishop of Canterbury from 668, was a vigorous upholder of Roman usage and made regulations concerning Sunday observance. Saturday loses its special significance while Sunday is confirmed in its unique status as the Church's sacred day.

Among the champions of Sunday observance in Ireland at this time were those reforming monks known as the 'Céilí Dé' or 'Culdees' (= the friends of God). These men set in motion a great spiritual movement in the Ireland of the eighth and ninth centuries. They are remembered not only for their very ascetic lives but also for the beauty of their nature poetry; for they were not only ascetics but aesthetes as well, and the poems written from their woodland hermitages may be said to anticipate the spirituality of St Francis.

The members of this reform movement insisted on a strict interpretation of the Sabbath rest. For example, servile work was forbidden in their communities from Vespers on Saturday until Monday morning. Monks were not supposed to accept food brought from a distance on Sunday, and, if accepted, it was to be given to the poor. Food prepared on Sunday would not be eaten. Only short journeys were allowed. This was to be strictly a day of worship and rest.[9]

The Cáin Domhnaigh

We now consider an important compilation concerning the observance of Sunday. It is the so-called *Cáin Domhnaigh* or 'Law of Sunday', which was composed about the beginning of the eighth century. The *Cáin* consists of three parts:
1) the *Epistil Ísú* or 'Epistle of Jesus'
2) anecdotes relating to violations of the Sabbath rest
3) the *Cáin* proper, a mainly legal treatise listing prohibitions and penalties pertaining to work and other activities on Sunday.

It is only in the first of these that we are presented with a really attractive vision of Sunday. As the title suggests, this treatise has an apocalyptic source. The claim that it was written by the Lord himself has its origin in an earlier document, the so-called *Carta Dominica*, an apocryphal work which was in circulation throughout Europe around this time. This document and its derivatives could be described as a piece of ecclesiastical propaganda to bolster Sunday observance throughout the Church. And so our Epistle begins with the claim that it was written by the Lord Jesus Christ himself, who wrote it in his own hand and had it placed on the altar of the apostle Peter in Rome in order to have Sunday kept holy for all time.

The *Epistil Ísú* has been beautifully translated by Máire Herbert in *Irish Biblical Apocrypha*, a work she edited with Fr Martin McNamara.[10] Here I quote a passage which describes the rewards awaiting those who faithfully observe the Lord's Day:

> The windows of heaven will be opened for them, and God will grant a blessing on themselves, on their dwellings, and on their lands, so that no poverty or hunger will affect a house in which Sunday is observed. Any prayer asked of God at the burial place of saints will be granted to those who maintain Sunday observance. They will inherit the earth here, and they will have heaven in the next life, and the Lord will make welcome their souls.

It then enumerates the great events in creation and redemption which were believed to have taken place on Sunday. For example, it was on this day that God created the light, that the Israelites crossed the Red Sea dry-shod, that the manna fell from heaven to provide food for God's people; it was also on this day that the Son of God was conceived in the womb of the Virgin Mary, that Jesus was baptised in the Jordan, and it was the day of his Transfiguration, Resurrection, and of the descent of the Holy Spirit on the apostles.

The Epistle surveys the whole history of salvation and looks forward to its completion at the end of the ages; for 'on a Sunday will be the general resurrection, when Christ will come to judge the living and the dead'. And, by way of conclusion, we are given this splendid description of the renewed creation: 'On a Sunday all created things will be renewed in a better and more beautiful form than they were fashioned in their first creation, when the stars of heaven will be like the moon, the moon like the sun, and the sun like the brightness of seven suns, as was the first light of the sun, before the sin of Adam.'

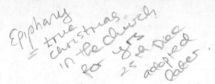

These are the reasons why Sunday should be observed. They express grateful remembrance of the wonderful works of God rather than fear of dire punishment (the negative aspect). What could be more positive than this statement: 'Even if there had not come from Jesus Christ this wondrous ⸱ ⸱⸱⸱⸱pt for the observance of Sunday, the day should be ⸱acred, revered, sanctified, and honoured, since ⸱ ⸱as the day on which all these miracles happened?'

Catechesis Celtica

We now turn to a group of texts known as th⸱ *Catechesis Celtica* (Celtic Catechesis). This consists of a colle⸱tion of homilies on various themes. One of these homilies dates from the late ninth or early tenth century. It is of Breton or Welsh origin but reflects a strong Irish influence.[11] In this homily we find an enumeration of the great works of God which, it was claimed, took place on a Sunday. It is reminiscent of the 'Epistle of Jesus' discussed above. We are told why Sunday is blessed above all other days. It reads like a list of beatitudes as each phrase begins with: 'The Day of the Lord is blessed because'.... Then it proceeds to declare that on this day God breathed a soul into Adam; on this day Abel offered gifts from his hand to God; Noah saw a light from out of the ark; the Israelites passed through the Red Sea; water flowed from the rock and the manna came down from heaven; on this day Joshua crossed the river Jordan; Abraham was visited by the angels; and so on. And then it passes to the New Testament. We are told that Sunday is blessed because on this day Christ was born, water was changed into wine in Galilee, and Jesus began his fast in the desert. It was the day of his Resurrection and of his sending the Holy Spirit at Pentecost. Finally, it is the day when the Lord will come again to judge the living and the dead.

Writing in the liturgical review *Worship*, Thomas O'Loughlin has provided a translation of this homily together with translations of two other homilies, one Breton, the other Anglo-Saxon, dating from the early ninth century.[12] The three texts are similar in genre and express the concern of the

Church at this period to instruct the Christian faithful on the true meaning of Sunday. They ex   it, in the words of the author, a 'joy and exultation over the Lord's Day stemming from it being the day of the *magnalia Dei* (the mighty works of   ) and their narration by the Church, rather than the dour abstinence/punishment themes of Sabbatarianism'.[13] Here we find beautiful expressions such as: 'Now, as the Mother of the Lord hold first place among all women, so amongst the rest of the   s of all the days, the Lord's Day is the greatest.' And the   in the note of exultation: 'The day of the Lord, O da   lessed day, venerable day, on which the people come tog   i to the Church.'

Sunday and salvation history

It is not to be supposed that all the miraculous happenings listed above literally took place on a Sunday. On reflection, however, what at first sight may appear fanciful and far-fetched, contains a profound truth. For what we are dealing with here is not chronology but theology. These listings of *mirabilia* or 'miracles' can be understood in the sense that all sacred history converges on, and is contained in the paschal mystery of the Passion, Death and glorification of Jesus. And this paschal mystery is celebrated not only once a year at Easter, but every Sunday, the Church's 'original feast-day'.[14]

A visual image of this is provided by the Celtic cross of which there is such a rich variety. They provide a catechesis in stone on the meaning of the paschal mystery. Various panels on both sides of the cross depict scenes from the Old and New Testaments. They represent key moments in the history of salvation. But the central figure is that of Christ on the Cross. He is the crucified one, the lamb of sacrifice; but he is also a figure of majesty, a king who reigns from the cross, the one who will come to judge the living and the dead. Is that not the whole mystery of salvation which we celebrate each Sunday and indeed at each Eucharist?

Sunday and sacraments

In the 'Epistle of Jesus', as well as in the homilies, there are implicit allusions to the sacraments. They are presented in the types and figures of the Old Testament. Baptism is prefigured in the crossing of the Red Sea, in the miraculous flow of water from the rock, in Joshua leading his people across the Jordan into the Promised Land.

The Eucharist is also included among the blessings of Sunday. In the 'Epistle of Jesus', we meet this intriguing phrase: 'On a Sunday Christ blessed the five loaves and two salmon, so that five thousand were fed by them, and they had twelve baskets of left-overs.' This substitution of 'salmon' (much revered in Celtic mythology) for the generic 'fish' gives the passage a distinctly Irish tone. Again we read in the Epistle: 'On a Sunday Christ made wine from water in Canaan of Galilee, at the wedding of John, the beloved disciple.' Surely this too is a reference to the Eucharist. And again, in the homily of the *Celtic Catechesis*, we can detect an allusion to the sacrifice of the Mass in the following 'blessing': 'The Day of the Lord is blessed because on that day Abel offered the gifts from his hands to God.' It also mentions the manna that rained down for forty days to feed the Israelites. And so baptism and Eucharist form part of the mystery of Sunday. Sunday is a sacramental day, recalling and reactivating the sacraments of Christian initiation.

Easter joy

We will now consider a seventh-century Irish liturgical book, the Antiphonary of Bangor. It was written towards the end of the seventh century in the monastery of Bangor on the southern shore of Belfast Lough. The monastery, founded by St Comgall in 555, became an important centre of learning and of missionary impulse. The great Columbanus was a monk there. This book, which contains antiphons, hymns, prayers and other texts, may have been the abbot's personal handbook for presiding at the monastic office.[15]

It is the second part of the Sunday morning office that

canticle

especially claims our attention. Here we have a liturgy of resurrection that is joyful and even exultant. It celebrates the Resurrection of Christ and our own sharing in that mystery; it also expresses the Church's faith in the mystery of the Holy Trinity.

The basic structure of the office consists of:
1) the canticle of Moses and the Israelites after the crossing of the Red Sea (Exodus 15), followed by a collect
2) the canticle of the three young men in the fiery furnace (Daniel 3), and a collect
3) Psalms 148-150, with collect
4) the Gospel and collect
5) hymn and collect
6) commemoration of the martyrs

It is almost certain that the Gospel referred to here is the Gospel of the Resurrection according to the four Gospels, one for each week. This is the belief of Fr Michael Curran in his exhaustive study of the Antiphonary of Bangor.[16] Here the Irish Church would have followed a fairly widespread tradition, the ultimate source of which is the fourth-century Jerusalem liturgy. As we learn from the pilgrim Egeria in her Diary, the Sunday morning vigil, celebrated at cockcrow, consisted of three psalms or canticles, each followed by a prayer. Then the Gospel of the Resurrection was read by the bishop. The office was concluded by another psalm and prayer.

Let us now try to imagine the scene as dawn breaks in the abbey church at Bangor. The abbot or presiding presbyter comes forward to the lectern and solemnly proclaims the Gospel of the Resurrection. The monks stand and listen with reverence; it was as though Christ was in their midst and addressing them in person.

Here is the first of the prayers which follows on the Gospel and is inspired by its message:

> Rejoicing at the return of light this day, let us offer praise and thanksgiving to Almighty God. We implore his mercy that he may grant us peace, tranquillity and joy

as we celebrate with solemn rite the day of the Lord's
resurrection; and, having enjoyed his loving protection
from the morning watch until nightfall, may we exult
with perpetual gladness. Through our Lord Jesus Christ.

Note the joyful tone of this prayer. The word 'exult'
(*exultantes*) occurs twice. And this joy of Sunday is a foretaste
of the perpetual gladness of heaven. The second prayer is in
the same mood:

> Celebrating the Lord's day, the beginning of our
> resurrection, with united hearts let us render fitting
> praise and thanksgiving to our Triune God, imploring
> his mercy that he may enable us to share both in mind
> and body in the resurrection of our Lord and Saviour,
> who lives with the Father and the Holy Spirit God for
> ever and ever.

Mention of the Trinity here is significant, and we shall return
to this theme. For the present let us note that this prayer
faithfully echoes the teaching of St Paul on our sharing in the
mysteries of Christ. Through faith and baptism we have died
with Christ and have risen with him. But what has been
realised already in an initial way must grow and achieve its full
perfection. We are called to share fully, body and soul, in the
glory of the Resurrection.

The third and fourth prayers are quite short, and so we
quote them one after the other:

> We implore the Lord, who rises from the dead at this
> hour of daybreak, that we too may rise to eternal life for
> ever and ever.
> At the dawn of day let us exult in the Lord, the rising
> author of life, who has conquered death; wherefore, may
> we always resist sin and walk in newness of life.

That final prayer uses the word 'exult' again. But it also

reminds us of the consequences of our being saved through the Death and Resurrection of Christ. The paschal mystery must become a reality in our lives. As St Paul declares: 'You must see yourselves as being dead to sin but alive for God in Christ Jesus.' (Rm 6:11)

Faith in the Trinity

Only in one of the prayers quoted above is there explicit mention of the Trinity. Elsewhere in the Sunday morning office, however, the doctrine of the Trinity is given prominence. We meet it in the hymn *Spiritus divinae lucis* (The Spirit of Divine Life), an extended eulogy of the Three Divine Persons and their unity.[17] It is an Irish composition, much influenced by the thought and language of the fourth-century Latin Christian writer Marius Victorinus. It is a strong affirmation of the dogma of the Trinity as three Persons in one substance. The following collect-prayer, which is also very trinitarian in tone, may have been intended for use with the hymn. We give it in the Latin original followed by a translation by Fr Placid Murray:

> *Sancte domine, inluminatio et salus vera credentibus, resurrectio dominicae claritatis, inlumina cor nostrum, ut trinitatis scientia et unitatis cognitione filii lucis et membra Christi ac templum sancti spiritus esse mereamur, qui regnas in saecula saeculorum.*

> Holy Lord,
> true light and salvation for believers,
> the resurrection of the Lord's glory,
> light up our heart,
> so that by knowing the Three and the One
> we may merit to be
> children of light, members of Christ and the temple of the Holy Spirit, you who reign for ever and ever.

It has been suggested that the concept of Sunday as the day of the Trinity originated in Ireland. J. A Jungmann writes:

21

'The beginning of such a conception of Sunday appears as early as the seventh century in Ireland.' He cites the Antiphonary of Bangor in support of this view. He notes that by the year 800 the fully developed Trinitarian Mass had appeared in the sacramentaries. This was first inserted in these texts by Alcuin (735-804), who was religious adviser to Charlemagne. Alcuin allotted the Trinitarian Mass to the Sunday within the weekly cycle of votive Masses.[18]

In the opinion of another German scholar, Willibrord Godel, OSB, Alcuin, in composing a votive Mass of the Trinity for Sundays, may have been directly inspired by the example of the Antiphonary of Bangor. He proposes this view in his study of Irish prayers in the early Middle Ages.[19] He notes the existence side by side in the Antiphonary of the *fides Trinitatis* and the Easter mystery. He discerns here the beginning of a process whereby the trinitarian motif gains ascendancy over the paschal mystery.

It is noteworthy that the old *Missale Romanum*, promulgated by Pope Pius V in 1570, contained only one preface for Sundays and that was the preface of the Trinity. For four hundred years, until the Missal of Pope Paul VI in 1970, this was the invariable formula. Now the emphasis has fundamentally changed. The reformed Missal gives us a choice of eight prefaces, nearly all of which stress the paschal character of Sunday. The old Trinitarian preface has been relegated to Trinity Sunday. Of the new formularies, only the last (No.8) has as its theme the Church united in the mystery of the Trinity.

While the emphasis is now rightly laid on the paschal mystery, we should not lose sight of the Trinitarian aspect of Sunday. The Holy Trinity, the central mystery of Christian faith and life, must be included in a total understanding of the Lord's Day. Here Irish tradition, and medieval piety in general, has still something of importance to teach us. This can enrich our spirituality of Sunday provided that we view the Trinity not as an abstract dogma but as a dynamic reality. What is implied here is the inner life of the Godhead, a communion of life and love. In this triune God we 'live and move and have our being'.

Sunday is indeed the Lord's Day, the day on which Christ by rising from the dead revealed himself as *Kyrios*. But Jesus spoke of himself not as the final goal of our lives but as 'the Way'. He is the Way, the 'Door', the Mediator of the new and eternal covenant. He is the way to the Father, the return journey to God. His kingdom is an eternal kingdom, but that kingdom he will ultimately hand over to the Father so that 'God may be all in all' (I Cor 15:28).

And so Christ, the incarnate Word, leads us beyond himself to the Father and into the life of the Trinity. And so it could be said that every Sunday is not only an Easter Sunday but also a Pentecost Sunday and a Trinity Sunday. The Holy Spirit is present and active in the assembled community. To celebrate Sunday is to open ourselves to the joy and inspiration of the Holy Spirit. It is through his power that we are enabled to profess our baptismal faith, to confess that 'Jesus is Lord'.

On Sunday we recall our baptism which made us sharers of the divine nature, children of God, members of Christ. It has been said that for Irish people the baptismal font is the real 'holy well' of the parish. It is our 'Tobar Domhnaigh', 'Sunday Well'. By the grace of baptism we are called to share in the life of the Blessed Trinity, to enter into a personal and intimate relationship with each of the Divine Persons. In the Catechism of the Catholic Church (260) we read: 'The ultimate end of the whole divine economy is the entry of God's creatures into the perfect unity of the Blessed Trinity.'

This life of communion in the inner life of the Godhead is further strengthened by participation in the Eucharist. Here at Sunday Mass we profess our baptismal faith. The eucharistic prayer, addressed to the Father, is the perfect expression of the Church's faith in the Trinity. In the celebration of the sacred mysteries, bread and wine are changed into the body and blood of Christ, and the Holy Spirit, who effects this change, makes of us participants 'one body, one spirit, in Christ'. Here remembrance and thanksgiving lead to the final outpouring of

doxology

praise in the great doxology: 'Through him, with him, in him, in the unity of the Holy Spirit, all honour and glory are yours, Almighty Father, for ever and ever.'

2
the mass in ancient ireland

From the time of St Patrick the Church in Ireland has
faithfully fulfilled the Lord's command: 'Do this in memory of
me.' It has been mindful of the apostle's words: 'Whenever
you eat this bread and drink this cup, you are proclaiming the
Lord's death until he comes' (I Cor 11:25).

The Mass has not changed. In its essentials it has remained
as it was bequeathed to us by the Lord himself at the Last
Supper. But the liturgy surrounding the mystery of faith has
undergone considerable development over the centuries. The
rites and prayers of the liturgy reveal the Church's
understanding of the eucharistic mystery at various times and
in different cultural milieus.[1]

If St Patrick (c.390-c.460) was not the first apostle of the
Christian faith in Ireland, he was without doubt the missionary
who had by far the greatest influence. As priest and bishop he
preached and baptised and offered the holy sacrifice.
Regrettably, we have no clear idea of the ritual shape and
content of the Mass in Ireland at the time of St Patrick or in
the centuries immediately following. We can surmise, however,
that in its main features it would have been similar to the kind
of liturgy practised throughout Gaul during this period. St
Patrick and some of his followers came from Britain whose
Church had close links with Gaul. It is reasonable to suppose
that they would have brought to Ireland the liturgical practices
with which they were familiar.[2]

So the Mass during the first centuries of Christianity in
Ireland would have been Gaulish or Gallican in type. We are
quite well informed about this kind of liturgy from various

sacramentaries such as the *Missale Gothicum* and the *Missale Gallicanum Vetus* (copied around the first half of the eighth century). One of the interesting features of the Gallican Mass was the large number and variety of prayers. Even the Eucharistic Prayer could vary from Sunday to Sunday. The anaphora was made up of independent successive pieces. The Institution narrative remained the same, but the other sections were variable.[3]

Mass in the Stowe Missal   800 AD

Here we shall try to reconstruct the Mass as set out in the earliest Irish missal that we have, the so-called Stowe Missal. It was compiled about the year 800. Its contents are probably older than that. Its place of origin may have been the monastery founded by Maelruain in Tallaght near Dublin or the monastery of St Ruadán in Lorrha, Co. Tipperary. Fr John Ryan SJ argues in favour of the latter location. It certainly has a connection with the monastery of Lorrha.[4] The name Stowe Missal is a misnomer as its connection with this English town is quite accidental. Our missal, which for a while was in the possession of the Duke of Buckingham, was catalogued at Stowe in 1819. It is now in the library of the Royal Irish Academy in Dublin.

The Missal contains the Ordinary of the Mass in Latin with some Irish rubrics. The original manuscript, which is the work of one scribe, has in places been written over by a later redactor bearing the name of Maelcáich. It thus witnesses to a state of transition. In addition to the Ordinary of the Mass it contains texts for a Mass of All the Saints, a Mass for Penitents and one for the dead. The Missal also has an interesting tract in Old Irish explaining in an allegorical fashion the significance of the rites and prayers of the Mass.

Description of the Mass

Let us now try to imagine, with the help of the Stowe Missal and other liturgical sources, the unfolding of a eucharistic celebration in the Ireland of the late eighth and early ninth

The Mass in Ancient Ireland

century. Not that the rite would have been the same in every church or locality. There was significant diversity in customs and traditions, but the liturgy as presented in the Stowe Missal may be regarded as fairly representative of the Mass rite that was in use throughout central and southern Ireland at this time.

The Mass begins with a prayer of penance followed by a litany of the saints. (From the start we note this predilection for the saints in Celtic liturgy.) This litany includes the apostles, the fathers of the Church and twenty-five Irish saints. There was a strong sense of the *communio sanctorum*, and a manifest devotion to the great Irish saints in the Celtic liturgy; and so their intercession was sought from the beginning of the eucharistic rite.[5]

Various prayers follow: the 'Prayer of Augustine', a humble acknowledgement of unworthiness, the 'Prayer of Ambrose', in the same vein, and a little petition sung at every Mass, 'May our prayer rise to the throne of your glory so that our requests may not return to us empty'. The Collect of the day follows; a special one is given for feasts of Christ and of Peter. Finally the '*Gloria in excelsis*', here called 'the Angelic hymn', is sung.

We have now arrived at the Liturgy of the Word. The first reading or epistle has a eucharistic theme. The passage is from I Cor 11:26-32, which begins: 'Whenever you eat this bread and drink this cup, you are proclaiming the Lord's death until he comes.'

Prayers, psalms or psalm verses follow the Epistle, and then a litany called 'the Supplication of St Martin for the people'. It is of Eastern origin and includes petitions for all human categories. Its antiquity is indicated by one of the requests 'for the most devout emperors and the whole Roman empire'. A rather incongruous prayer in an Irish monastery of this period! But there are other more relevant petitions for peace and tranquillity, for pilgrims, penitents, catechumens, and for those who carry out works of mercy in the Church. The two orations that follow are of the kind known as *apologiae*, earnest protestations of unworthiness on the part of the priest which were a feature of Western liturgies from the eighth to the tenth centuries.

It is at this point that the chalice is 'half uncovered'. The wine mixed with water would have been poured in at the beginning of the Mass. The celebrant now sings three times the verse of Psalm 140: 'Direct my prayer like incense in your sight; may the raising of my hands be like an evening sacrifice.' The first veil is then removed from the chalice. Then the priest sings three times: 'Come, Lord, almighty Sanctificator, and bless this sacrifice prepared for you.'

After these various prayers and symbolic rites we have arrived at the Gospel. Although not described here, we can imagine an imposing procession with the singing of the Alleluia, followed by the veneration of the Gospel book. The text, like that chosen for the epistle, has a eucharistic theme. It is from John 6:51-57: 'I am the living bread which has come down from heaven. Anyone who eats this bread will live for ever; and the bread that I shall give is my flesh for the life of the world.'

To recreate the scene it may help to have a visual image of the Gospel book used for the liturgy. The most famous of these is the Book of Kells, which, composed in the late eighth or early ninth centuries, is contemporaneous with the Stowe Missal. It is a Latin copy of the four Gospels clearly intended for liturgical use. Also, because of the beauty of its ornamentation, it is likely that it was displayed open on the altar during ceremonies.[6] Not all the Gospel books would have been as sumptuous as the Book of Kells, or as technically perfect as the earlier Book of Durrow, but the general standard of workmanship was very high during this period. There is no doubt but that the Irish Church had a very high regard for the word of God, and this is reflected in the beauty of the manuscripts.

We may assume that the presiding minister would have preached on this Gospel text. The missal is silent about this but provides us with a 'Gregorian prayer over the Gospel'. Such prayers were customary at the time. This one, as the name suggests, is taken from the Gregorian Sacramentary. Then comes the profession of faith according to the Nicene

Creed. There are just a few slight differences from the text as we know it.

We now come to the Offertory Rite. This begins with the removal of the second veil from the chalice which is now fully revealed. And what a splendid sight this must have been! Again, it may help us to imagine some beautiful example of Celtic art such as the Ardagh chalice or the Derrynaflan chalice (8th-9th centuries). Of the former, Daphne Pochin Mould has written: 'The Ardagh chalice, now preserved in the National Museum in Dublin, seems, in the glitter and perfection of its workmanship, to crystallise and bring down to earth all the romance of the legends of the Holy Grail.'[7] Nothing was too precious to contain the wine that, in the course of the Mass, would become the sacred blood of Christ.

Now the priest sings the psalm verse three times: 'Show us, Lord, your mercy and grant us your salvation', while he holds the chalice aloft. There follow some Offertory prayers. One is addressed to Christ himself, and beseeches him who has suffered, died and risen again, to remember the souls of all our dear departed ones, 'whose names we recite, and those whom we do not recite but are recited by you in the Book of Life'. There follow further prayers and a further mention of the faithful who have gone before us, the souls of bishops, priests and deacons, relatives, 'our boys and girls', and penitents. May the Eucharist profit them all unto salvation.

After this rather elaborate Offertory Rite we have reached the central portion of the Mass, the Eucharistic Prayer. Here the reader may feel more 'at home', since the formula presented here is the old Roman Canon, familiar to us today as the first Eucharistic Prayer. It begins with the dialogue before the Preface: '*Sursum corda*', 'Lift up your hearts', and the reply, '*Habemus ad Dominum*', 'We have lifted them up to the Lord'. Then the invitation to give thanks to the Lord. The Preface is a paean of ecstatic praise of the Holy Trinity, which also gratefully brings to mind the Incarnation and Redemption. It is a splendid composition which merits quotation. Here, with slight adaptations, I have followed Fr John Ryan's version from the article already cited.[8]

> Father, all-powerful and ever-living God, we do well always and everywhere to give you thanks . . . you with your only-begotten Son and the Holy Spirit, are one and immortal, God incorruptible and unchangeable, God invisible and faithful, God wonderful and worthy of praise, God strong and worthy of honour, God most high and august, God living and true, God wise and powerful, God holy and beautiful, God noble and good, God venerable and peace-making, God beautiful and sincere, God pure and kind, God blessed and just, God good and holy; not in the oneness of a single person but in the Trinity of one substance. We believe you, we bless you, we adore you and praise your name for ever and ever, by whom is the salvation of the world, the life of men/women, the resurrection of the dead.

This concludes with the '*Sanctus*' and a '*Post-Sanctus*', in which we are given an additional motive for praise and thanksgiving: 'Blessed is he who came from heaven that he might dwell on earth, was made man that he might blot out the sins of the flesh, was made a victim that, through his Passion, he might grant eternal life to those who believe.'

After the '*Te igitur*', a prayer asking for acceptance of the sacrifice, there comes an extended '*Memento*' of the living and the dead. This includes petitions for fine weather, the crops, peace, the safety of kings and rulers, for travellers, for the sick and those in pain that the divine mercy may deign to heal them, and for those whom the Lord has summoned from the darkness of this world. Earnest intercessory prayer is one of the features of this liturgy.

We move now to the Institution narrative and moment of consecration. There is a rubric in the Leabhar Breac (speckled book) which directs that when the priest says, 'Jesus took bread', he bows three times. After the offering of the chalice he chants three times, 'Have mercy on me, O God', and he takes three steps backwards and forwards. There is evidently a trinitarian symbolism here. As for the people, they kneel in silence during the 'perilous prayer' (i.e. the words of consecration), so called because of fear of any irreverence during these sacred moments. Of interest is the formula spoken over the wine: '*Hic est enim calix sancti sanguinis mei*', 'This is the chalice of my holy blood.'

At the conclusion of the words, 'As often as you do this, you will do it in memory of me', there is the additional phrase, borrowed from the Ambrosian liturgy: 'You will proclaim my Passion, you will announce my Resurrection, you will hope for my Advent, until I come to you again from heaven.'

Of special interest in this Irish version of the Roman Canon is the commemoration of the saints. These were incorporated within the Memento for the dead. The Stowe Missal has invocations to a great number of saints, beginning with biblical saints from the Old and New Testaments; then the first martyrs and Desert Fathers, followed by such great Western saints as Martin of Tours and Pope St Gregory the Great. There is added an extensive list (longer than that found at the beginning of the Mass) of native Irish saints. John Hennig, a specialist in Celtic liturgy and devotion to the saints in Ireland, claims that the Irish Church played a significant role in introducing Old Testament saints to the liturgy of the Western Church, as well as in promoting devotion to the holy men and women of one's own land. There is here not only a recognition of the saints of the Old Covenant, but also the intention to draw a parallel between Israel and Ireland.[9] Corresponding with Abraham, Moses, David, Elijah and others, we have Patrick, Ailbe, Senan, Finbarr, Declan *et alii*. The names are predominantly male, but include Brigid, Ita, and three other Irish virgins not easy to identify. The prayer is concluded with the commemoration of all the dead 'from Adam to the present day'. For these and for all who sleep in Christ may the Lord grant a place of 'light, happiness and peace'.

At the final doxology, 'Through him, with him, in him...', the host is raised above the chalice and the under part lowered into it. Then the priest sings the psalm verse three times: 'May your mercy be upon us, O Lord, since we have hoped in you.' This is followed by a rubric in Irish which reads: 'It is here the bread is broken.' This is the rite of fraction which takes place *before* the Lord's Prayer, and not after it as is the Roman practice. In the Mass treatise appended to the missal we find this explanation: 'The Host on the paten is Christ's flesh on the tree of the cross. The fraction on the paten is the breaking of Christ's body with the nails of the cross. The meeting wherewith the two halves meet after the fraction is the figure of the wholeness of Christ's body after the Resurrection.'

It seems that another more elaborate rite of fraction was practised in the Irish Church around this time. It may have taken place at a later point in the ceremony, before the Communion. The same old Irish tract referred to above gives a description as well as a symbolic explanation of this ritual.[10] According to the tract, the number of particles into which the host is divided depends on the importance of the occasion. For example, on ordinary Sundays it is divided into nine parts, for 'the oblation of Sunday is a figure of the nine households of heaven and the nine grades of the Church'. The common division on ordinary days is five parts. For the three greatest solemnities, Easter, Pentecost and Christmas, the number of particles amounts to sixty-five. This description of the divisions of the host is very much the pattern of the Orthodox rite seen in the Prothesis. The very large paten found with the Derrynaflan chalice may well have been used for such an elaborate fraction.

Now the particles are arranged in the form of a cross within a circle. The different parts represent different categories of people. Here we may quote from the tract itself:

> What is upwards of the shaft pertains to bishops, the
> cross-piece on the left to priests, that on the right to
> lesser clerics; that from the cross-piece down to

anchorites and penitents; that which is in the left upper angle to young students of the priesthood; the right upper to innocent children, the left to people of repentance, the right lower to folk lawfully married and to those who have not yet put their hands to it.

The last phrase is obscure. Patrick O'Reilly, from whose article I have taken this translation, believes that it refers to those who have not yet married. Diarmuid Ó Laoghaire, on the other hand, favours the rendering: 'people who have not yet gone to communion before'. It seems that the Irish term for receiving communion implied *putting out the hand* to receive the sacred host.[11] While scholars may differ on a point of interpretation, they are at one in highlighting the underlying symbolism of the Celtic *Fractio*. It is a symbol of the unity of the Church and of the incorporation of all categories of people within it, and of their inclusion in the eucharistic sacrifice. 'Again the stress is on the unity of all, however different, in the one Body of Christ' (Ó Laoghaire). 'In the early Celtic Church the liturgy took account of those assisting at Mass and not of the celebrant only. Each section of the community was catered for and the Mass was a true community celebration' (O'Reilly).

Then comes the *Pater noster* or Lord's Prayer with its introduction and embolism, 'Deliver us, Lord'. A greeting of peace follows: 'The peace and love of our Lord Jesus Christ, and the communion of all the saints be always with us.' It appears that at this point the kiss of peace was exchanged. The prayer that follows develops the theme of peace, 'Lord Jesus Christ, you said to your apostles...'. Then the *commixtio* or commingling: 'May this mingling of the body and blood of Christ bring eternal life to us who receive it'.

The Communion rite was characterised by a spirit of deep reverence combined with genuine joyfulness. We hear of a threefold bow performed by the communicants as they approached the altar. Sacramental participation required deep interior dispositions. A much-quoted passage in the Leabhar Breac directs: 'Let this be your intention: Let the particle of the host which you receive be reverenced as a portion of Christ on the cross. Thus there must be in each one's life some cross of trouble or hardship, uniting him/her with the Lord's crucified body.'[12] Also in the Leabhar Breac we read: 'In going to meet it, it is not just a portion of the holy body one consumes, but it is the very body of Mary's Son we all eat at the altar.'[13] Communicants approached the altar with awe and reverence, but also with eager anticipation and joy. The Communion antiphons give witness to this spirit of joy; they also suggest strongly that the laity as well as the clergy received from the chalice. Apart from the Communion antiphons that we find in the Stowe Missal, similar lists are contained in other Irish compilations such as the the Antiphonary of Bangor, the Books of Deer, Dimma and Mulling. It seems reasonable to infer that Communion chants of this kind were a characteristic and popular element of Irish eucharistic piety. Here are some examples from the Stowe Missal.[14]

> The King of Heaven, with peace, alleluia!
> Deep fragrance of life, alleluia!
> Sing a new chant, alleluia!
> All you saints approach, alleluia!
> Come, eat my bread, alleluia!
> and drink the wine that I have prepared for you, alleluia!
> He who eats my flesh and drinks my blood, alleluia!
> The same abides in me, alleluia!
> This sacred body and blood of the Lord and Saviour, alleluia!
> Take for yourselves unto eternal life, alleluia!

The reiterated alleluia gives these Scripture verses an added quality of Easter joy. One of the antiphons, '*Omnes sancti venite*', ('All you saints approach') puts one in mind of the great eucharistic hymn, '*Sancti venite*', which is found in the Antiphonary of Bangor. Because of its great antiquity and doctrinal richness, it will be considered at length in the next chapter. The Mass now draws to a close. There follow two post-communion prayers, both taken from the Roman liturgy. The second of them reads as follows:

> We give you thanks, Lord, holy Father, almighty and eternal God, who have filled us with the communion of the body and blood of your Son. We implore your mercy, Lord, that this your sacrament may not be for us a cause for punishment, but a saving intercession for forgiveness. May it be the washing away of our sins, the strength of the weak, a firm foundation against the danger of the world. May this communion deliver us from our faults, and make us sharers in heavenly joy. Through Christ our Lord.

On this humble, penitential and trusting note, the celebration has reached its conclusion. There only remains the simple dismissal: '*Missa acta est; in pace*', 'The Mass is ended; [go] in peace'.

3
'Sancti venite'
an ancient eucharistic hymn

All too seldom nowadays do we hear, either in Latin or in the vernacular, this ancient and beautiful hymn which expresses so well the eucharistic faith and devotion of the early Irish Church.[1] The 'Sancti venite' is reputed to be the oldest eucharistic hymn of the Western Church. It is found in the Antiphonary of Bangor. In his comprehensive study of this book Fr Michael Curran judges this hymn to be an authentically Irish composition dating from the sixth century. He esteems it to be 'a eucharistic hymn of fine theological and devotional quality'.[2] The Franciscan scholar, Felim Ó Briain, praised its 'robust and simple faith'.[3]

Not only is it the most ancient eucharistic hymn of the Western Church, it also appears to be the *only* such hymn for several centuries. In their study of devotion to the Eucharist in the early centuries and Middle Ages, the Belgian scholars Chanoine Baix and Dom Cyril Lambot maintained that it served as the only eucharistic hymn until the thirteenth century, the age which saw such a splendid flowering of eucharistic hymnody. Like the early primrose, it is a promise and foretaste of spring. Comparing it with the later masterpiece, the 'Pange lingua', attributed to St Thomas Aquinas (1225-74), they concur with Dom Cabrol that, while it does not quite match the profound theology of the 'Pange lingua', it is superior by reason of its 'truth and simplicity of accent'.[4]

The 'Sancti venite' was widely used and highly esteemed in the Irish Church. According to a legend recorded in the Leabhar Breac, it was first sung by angels when St Patrick was visiting his disciple Seachnall (Secundinus). They heard it while going round the cemetery at Dunshaughlin, Co. Meath, at the time the oblation was being made in the church. More importantly, we learn that: 'Wherefore from this time forward this hymn is sung in Ireland *when one goes to Christ's Body*.'[5]

The Antiphonary of Bangor prefaces the hymn with the directive: 'When priests receive Communion'. It would be wrong to infer, however, that the hymn concerned only the clergy. On the contrary, as John Hennig has pointed out, it 'actually refers to the communion of *all the faithful*', and he supports this assertion by comparisons with the post-communion prayers of the Antiphonary as well as the Communion hymn in St Gall 1394.[6]

It is now time to consider the hymn itself. Both Latin text and prose rendering have been provided by Daphne Pochin Mould in her fine book, *The Celtic Saints, Our Heritage* (pp. 56-58).[7] The author characteristically observes that the hymn 'puts into words what the Ardagh chalice expresses in the shimmering patterns of Celtic art'.

1) *Sancti venite*　　　　Approach, you who are holy,
　 Christi corpus sumite　Receive the body of Christ,
　 Sanctum bibentes　　Drinking the sacred blood
　 quo redempti sanguinem.　By which you were redeemed.

2) *Salvati Christi*　　　Saved by the body
　 Corpore et sanguine,　And blood of Christ
　 a quo refecti　　　Now nourished by it,
　 laudes dicamus Deo.　Let us sing praises unto God.

3) *Hoc sacramento*　　By this sacrament
　 Corporis et sanguinis　Of the body and blood
　 omnes exuti　　　All are rescued
　 ab inferno faucibus.　From the power of death.

4) *Dator salutis*　　　The giver of salvation,
　 Christus, filius Dei　Christ, the Son of God,

mundum salvavit	Redeemed the world
per crucem et sanguinem.	By his cross and blood.

5) *Pro universis*
   immolatus Dominus
   Ipse sacerdos
   existit et hostia.

For the whole world
the Lord is offered up;
He is at the same time
High priest and victim.

6) *Lege preceptum*
   immolari hostias
   qua adumbrantur
   divina mysteria.

In the Law it is commanded
to immolate victims;
By it were foreshadowed
These sacred mysteries.

7) *Lucis indultor*
   et salvator omnium
   praeclaram sanctis
   largitus est gratiam.

The giver of all light,
and the saviour of all,
Now bestows upon the holy
An exceeding grace.

8) *Accedant omnes*
   pura mente creduli,
   sumant aeternam
   salutis custodiam.

Let all approach
In the pure simplicity of faith;
Let them receive the eternal
Preserver of their souls.

9) *Sanctorum custos*
   Rector quoque Dominus,
   vitae perennis
   largitor credentibus.

The guardian of the saints,
The supreme Ruler and Lord,
The bestower of eternal life,
On those who believe in him.

10) *Coelestem panem*
   dat esurientibus
   de fonte vivo
   praebet sitientibus.

To the hungry he gives to eat
of the heavenly food;
To the thirsty he gives to drink
From the living fountain.

11) *Alpha et Omega*
   Ipse Christus Dominus
   venit, venturus
   iudicare homines.

The Alpha and Omega,
Our Lord Christ himself
Now comes who shall one day com
To judge all humankind.

Commentary

It is a welcoming hymn, requiring of those who approach the altar nothing more than a simple, strong, vital faith. It could be said that two Scripture texts determine the right attitude of mind and heart in those who come to receive the body and blood of Christ. There is firstly Jesus' invitation to his disciples at the Last Supper: 'Take it and eat it, this is my body…. Drink from it, all of you, for this is my blood' (Mt 26:26); then there is Paul's admonition: 'Everyone is to examine himself/herself, and only then eat from the bread and drink from the cup' (I Cor 11:28). Both the welcoming words of Jesus and the cautionary words of Paul are complementary. The Church over the centuries has stressed now this, now that aspect. There is a balance to be maintained here. If in the past there has been an exaggerated awe and fear on the part of lay Christians, keeping them away from sacramental communion, the tendency in our own time may be to adopt an all-too-casual approach. In this eucharistic hymn there appears to be just the right blend of deep reverence and a confident assurance of being welcome at the table of the Lord.

It must not be thought that the '*sancti*' of the first stanza applies to saints in the strict sense, i.e. exceptionally holy people. Rather, the reference is to the People of God in general, and to this eucharistic assembly in particular. They are the '*plebs sancta*', God's 'holy people'. We can understand the term in the Pauline sense. When Paul addressed his letters to the 'saints' of Rome, Corinth or Philippi, he had in mind the whole community of believers. Many of them were far from being saintly in their behaviour, but they had accepted the Gospel message and had been *sanctified* by the grace of baptism. Through faith, conversion and baptism, they had been incorporated into Christ, the Holy One of God. They had received the Spirit of holiness. This holy and redeemed people is now invited to come and take the body of Christ and to drink his holy blood.

This note of welcome is characteristic not only of this hymn but of the Communion antiphons in general such as we find them in the Stowe Missal and elsewhere. Take, for example, this antiphon, inspired by the Wisdom literature: 'Come, eat my bread, alleluia, and drink the wine that I have mixed for you, alleluia.'[8] In places the hymn seems to echo these antiphons. We also find similarities in other liturgies, as, for example, in the Communion chant, '*Venite populi*':

> Come, people, and partake of the sacred banquet of the immortal mystery. Let us approach in fear and faith, with hand purified by penance, and communicate with this gift. For the Lamb of God is offered by us in sacrifice to the Father. Him let us adore; to him alone let us give glory, singing with the angels, Alleluia.[9]

In stanza two we hear a strong echo of a Communion antiphon which is found frequently in other Celtic liturgical documents. The antiphon goes: '*Refecti Christi corpore et sanguine tibi semper, Domine, dicamus, alleluia*' ('Refreshed by the body and blood of Christ, let us always cry alleluia to you, Lord'). Interestingly, in the Book of Dimma, the Book of Mulling, the Book of Deer and in the Stowe Missal, it is given as part of the 'Order for communicating the sick'.[10] This relationship with the sick and infirm implies that the Eucharist is a sacrament of healing, not just a reward for the good. It is the 'medicine [*pharmacon*] of immortality'.

It can be inferred from the first three stanzas that the lay faithful as well as the clergy received Communion under the forms of bread and wine. This was the normal practice of the Church during the first centuries and would still have been the case when this hymn was composed. In the ancient Latin hymn, '*Audite omnes*', written by Secundinus (Seachnall) in honour of St Patrick, there is this revealing phrase: 'He drinks heavenly wine from the heavenly cups, and gives God's people the spiritual cup to drink.'[11] Of stanzas four to seven Michael Curran writes: 'Here the Eucharist is related to the sacrifice of Christ on the cross, and to the sacrifices of the Old Law which foreshadowed the sacred mysteries.'[12] In the opening line of stanza four our Lord is described as '*dator salutis*', 'giver of salvation'. We recall Jesus' words to the Samaritan woman: 'If only you knew the *gift of God*' (Jn 4:10). He is the giver of the living water, of the bread from heaven, of the Spirit. He is the giver of redemption, that supreme gift of which St Paul exclaims: 'Thanks be to God for his gift that is beyond all telling' (II Cor 9:15). In this same stanza we are reminded that this redemption was achieved '*per crucem et sanguinem*', 'by his cross and blood'. Christ died once for all on the cross, and that sacrifice cannot be repeated. But the Eucharist is the '*memoria passionis ejus*', 'the memorial of his Passion', and not only of his Passion, but of his Death and Resurrection as well, indeed of the whole paschal mystery which is recalled and made present in the sacramental mystery.

'*Mundum salvavit*', 'He saved the world'. We note the universalism of this hymn. What is affirmed here is reiterated in stanza five: '*pro universis*', 'for the whole world the Lord is offered up'. Again in stanza seven we meet the phrase, '*Salvator omnium*', 'Saviour of all people'. Here is a breadth of vision that faithfully reflects the universalism of the Gospel: 'And when I am lifted up from the earth, I shall draw all people to myself' (Jn 12:32). The blood of the covenant is shed 'for you and for all'. In the second of the eucharistic prayers there occurs the phrase: 'For our sakes he opened his arms on the cross', a gesture interpreted by the Church Fathers as an act of embracing the whole world.

In stanza five Christ is presented as both priest and victim. He is the High Priest of the new and eternal covenant, and he is the Lamb of Sacrifice. In what has been called the 'High Priestly prayer' of Jesus at the Last Supper, the meaning of Christ's Passion and Death is declared: 'For their sakes I consecrate myself' (Jn 17:19). Jesus offers himself in sacrifice and intercedes for his people. In the Letter to the Hebrews it is as our mediator and high priest that Jesus, through his Death, Resurrection and Ascension, enters into the sanctuary and into the presence of the Father. He is our priest from the moment of his Incarnation, and he is also the 'Lamb of God

41

who takes away the sin of the world' (Jn 1:29). John the evangelist is at pains to show that Jesus is the fulfilment of the Old Testament figure of the paschal lamb, that lamb of which St Paul exclaims: 'Christ our Pasch is sacrificed'. Priest and victim: we have a visual representation of this dual role in the ancient and weather-worn Celtic cross on the Rock of Cashel where the divine victim is shown wearing a long priestly robe.

The Fathers of the Church loved to explain in allegorical fashion how the Christian mysteries were prefigured in the Old Testament 'types'. Thus the sacrifice of Christ is prefigured in the sacrifices of Abel, Abraham and Melchisedech, as we recall in the Old Roman canon of the Mass. The great medieval eucharistic hymn already referred to, the '*Pange lingua*', sung at the Holy Thursday Mass, expresses the same idea: '*Tantum ergo sacramentum veneremur cernui/Et antiquum documentum novo cedat ritui*'; 'Let us therefore humbly reverence so great a sacrament. Let the old types depart and give way to the new'. ('Types and shadows have their ending/Now a newer rite appears').

At this point it may be worthwhile to list all the titles and attributes addressed to Christ in the course of the hymn: Giver of salvation (stanza four), giver of life and grace (stanza seven), giver of the heavenly bread and living water (stanza ten). Clearly for the hymn-writer Christ is the fount of life and source of all good. Of stanzas eight to ten Fr Curran writes: 'Through reception of the heavenly bread and living Fountain with the proper dispositions of faith and purity of intention, the Lord bestows his salvation, protection and eternal life.'[13]

Stanza eight begins with '*Accedant omnes*', 'Let all approach'. The use of the word '*accedere*' suggests an association with the great eucharistic Psalm 33(34). This psalm was very popular in the fourth century as a Communion chant. It was chosen chiefly because of the verse '*Gustate et videte*', 'Taste and see that the Lord is good'. But an earlier verse in the psalm was also understood in a eucharistic sense, and this was: '*Accedite ad eum et illuminamini*', 'Approach him and be enlightened'. St Augustine was fond of quoting this verse in a eucharistic context. It was very appropriate that it should be sung during a Communion procession. In the rite of Milan there is a Communion chant, known as the *transitorium*, which goes as follows: 'Approach the altar of God. Purify your hearts and be filled with the Holy Spirit, receiving the body and blood of Christ for the remission of sins.'

In the second-last stanza, there are echoes of St John's Gospel: 'I am the bread of life. No one who comes to me will ever hunger; no one who believes in me will ever thirst' (6:35). In the second couplet ('To the thirsty he gives drink from the living water'), there appears to be an allusion to Christ's discourse with the Samaritan woman at the well of Sychar. Interestingly Fr Curran draws our attention to a link with the teaching of St Columbanus. He says: 'The whole of Columban's Instruction 13 is a development of this theme: Christ is the bread and fountain of life, whom we are invited to eat and drink. He is not speaking specifically of the Eucharist, but it is not far from his thought.'[14] We are fortunate to have a reading from this Instruction in volume 3 of the Divine Office, (p. 473: Thursday of the twenty-first week of the year). The relevant passage reads: 'My brethren, let us follow this calling, with which we are called, not only to the fountain of living water, but also of eternal life, yes, and the fount of glory; for from him came all these things, wisdom and life and light eternal.'

The last stanza sounds an eschatological note. Christ is here identified as Alpha and Omega. It has been suggested that these letters, the first and last of the Greek alphabet, may have been impressed on the altar breads of the Irish Church at this time. They lead us back to the closing section of the Book of Revelation: 'I am the Alpha and Omega, the beginning and the end. I will give water from the well of life to anybody who is thirsty' (21:6). Also, in our association of ideas, we cannot fail to recall the words spoken at the Easter Vigil as the paschal candle is blessed: 'Christ yesterday and today, the beginning and the end, Alpha and Omega; all time belongs to him and all ages. To him be glory and power through every age and for ever. Amen.'

In the Eucharist the Church proclaims the death of the Lord 'until he comes'. The Eucharist points beyond the present reality to the *eschaton*, the final fulfilment in the *parousia* or Second Coming. It is the sign, pledge and foretaste of eternal life. When Christ comes again, it will be to judge the living and the dead. This has always been an awesome thought, especially for medieval men and women. But here the note of impending judgment is sounded lightly and unobtrusively at the end of a hymn which is essentially a lyrical affirmation of eucharistic faith and Christian hope. For the one who is to be our judge is the one who came to save us.

Popular versions

There are a number of English vernacular versions. A three-strophe rendering appears in the *Veritas Hymnal*, titled 'Come and Take the Flesh of Christ', and it is one that could easily be learnt by the average congregation. Another good version, titled 'Come Christ's Beloved', with melody by James Walsh and arrangement by Anthony Greening, is given in *New Hymns for all Seasons* (Geoffrey Chapman). Finally, we have the version printed below. It expresses very well the thought and spirit of the original. The translation is by J.M. Neale (1818-66), and it has been put to a traditional Irish melody. The hymn is printed in *Praise the Lord* (melody edition, revised and enlarged, London: Chapman, 1974):

> Draw nigh and take the body of your Lord,
> And drink with faith the blood for you outpoured.
> Saved by his body, hallowed by his blood,
> With souls refreshed we render thanks to God.
>
> Salvations's giver, Christ, the only Son,
> By his dear cross and blood the victory won.
> Offered was he for greatest and for least,
> Himself the victim and himself the priest.

Victims were offered by the law of old,
Which in a type celestial mysteries told.
He, the ransomer from death and light from shade,
Now gives his holy grace his saints to aid.

Approach ye then with faithful hearts sincere,
And take the pledges of salvation here.
He, that in this world rules his saints, and shields,
To all believers life eternal yields.

With heavenly bread makes them that hunger whole,
Gives living waters to the thirsting soul.
O Judge of all, our only Saviour thou,
In this thy feast of love be with us now.

4
from age to age

In chapter two we attempted a reconstruction of the Mass rite according to Celtic usage. The period was that of the end of the eighth and beginning of the ninth century. It was towards the close of what has been called the Golden Age of the Irish Church. But this tranquil era was followed by the invasions of the Norsemen in the course of the ninth and tenth centuries. The ensuing havoc and destruction contributed to a serious decline in religious life. But even at this darkest hour the Mass continued to be celebrated not only on Sundays but on weekdays as well.[1]

We pass now to the twelfth century, a period of renewal and reconstruction for the Irish Church. Some great reforming churchmen appeared, the most prominent being St Malachy who became Archbishop of Armagh in 1129. As well as initiating a number of reforming synods, he introduced the Cistercians and Augustinian canons to Ireland. He was a close friend of the great St Bernard of Clairvaux. He sought to lead the Irish Church into closer conformity with Rome in matters ecclesiastical and liturgical.

Every great reform in the Church is a story of loss and gain. A great synod held at Cashel in 1172 introduced some very necessary reforms, but it also spelt the end of much that was traditional in Celtic religious culture. It directed that the use of the English Church be followed in this country in all religious observances. This marked the decline and eventual disappearance of the Celtic rite.

With the introduction of these reforms and the coming of the religious orders from the Continent, first the monks and canons and then the mendicant orders in the thirteenth century, new forms of liturgy began to appear. They were basically Roman in type but offering interesting variants. Liturgy had not yet become fixed and uniform as was to be the situation in the centuries following the Council of Trent (1545-63).

What is not generally known is that from about this time the so-called Sarum rite came to be known and practised in this country. To what extent this is the case is not quite clear, but there is evidence for its use throughout Ireland. The rite derives its name from Salisbury in England. The cathedral church of this diocese enjoyed great prestige. While its liturgy was basically Roman in character, it differed in matters of ceremonial, calendar days, arrangement of readings and selection of prayers. The ceremonial was elaborate and dramatic with a propensity for processions. Such exuberance presented a marked contrast with Roman sobriety. The Sarum rite was widely used throughout England, and the first evidence for its use in this country is at Christ Church, Dublin. Here it was in use until the time of the Reformation. It provided some of the material later incorporated in the Book of Common Prayer.[2]

There is one liturgical practice associated with the Sarum rite which is of special interest. This has to do with the so-called 'Easter sepulchre', one of the most popular features of the Easter ceremonies. It enacted the symbolic burial of Christ in the tomb and his return from the dead on Easter morning. In what follows I give a brief account of the rite as carried out in St Patrick's Cathedral, Dublin, around the middle of the fourteenth century.[3]

On Good Friday, after Vespers, the Cross and a consecrated Host, the *Corpus Dominicum,* were carried in procession through the darkened church to a tomb representing the holy sepulchre. The priests went barefooted. The sepulchre was situated in the north side of the chancel. Clergy and choir alternated in the singing of the Scripture texts. All lights were extinguished except those in front of the sepulchre. The Host, carried in a pyx, and the Cross (both had been kissed by the people during the liturgy) were reverently laid within it. The Host was incensed and adored. Then on Easter morning before the office of Matins, a solemn procession, led by two senior priests, went to the tomb. The Host was carried back with great solemnity to its place in the tabernacle, the Cross carried aloft in procession. The church bells rang out, a prayer that all might share in the Resurrection was said, and all the congregation 'joyfully adored the Cross'.[4]

Describing the same rite in England, Eamon Duffy declares that 'the sepulchre and its ceremonies were the principal vehicle for the Easter proclamation'. It is one that left a deep mark on the minds of the laity as well as on the structure of many parish churches where examples of the Easter sepulchre are still to be found in the recesses of the north side of the chancel.[5]

Eucharistic faith

The Eucharist is a multi-faceted reality: memorial, sacrifice of Christ and his Church, renewal of the covenant, thanksgiving, sacred meal, koinonia or sharing, sign and pledge of the heavenly banquet. In the course of time, religious faith and sensibility have been drawn to particular aspects of the mystery. During the early and later Middle Ages, and indeed in the centuries following, the Irish Church, in line with other Western countries, has been strongly attracted by the sacrificial character of the Mass and the doctrine of the Real Presence.

Let us consider the sacrificial aspect first. Here the very name for the Mass in Irish is revealing. The word 'aifreann' (Mass) is from the Old Irish, 'oifrend', which in turn comes from the Latin *offerenda*. It denotes offering and sacrifice. Historically, there seems to be a link here with the Offertory Rite which took place at the beginning of Mass. In Milan this rite was accompanied by the singing of the chant known as *Offerenda*.[6]

In the allegorical explanations of the Mass rite that we find in the Stowe Missal and the Leabhar Breac, the tendency is to relate almost every moment and incident of the celebration to the Passion and sacrificial Death of Christ. Such a tendency is a feature of medieval piety in general, but it is particularly marked in Irish devotion. Moreover it remained part of the Catholic consciousness down to our own times. The seventeenth-century Franciscan friar, Geoffrey Keating, in his devotional treatise on the Mass, asks the question: 'How should the Christian hear the Mass?' And he answers: 'First of all, let him think that he is as it were on the way to Calvary . . . in the company of the Blessed Virgin Mary, John of the Breast ('Eoin Bruinne') and Mary Magdalen.'[7]

The other constant of eucharistic faith and devotion is the doctrine of the Real Presence. (We use this term in the awareness of the reality of other modes of Christ's presence in the Eucharist – in the word proclaimed, in the priest and assembled community. Christ's presence in the consecrated bread and wine might better be termed 'the real substantial presence'.)

Evidence of strong belief in the reality of Christ's presence in the Eucharist is available from early times. The homily on the Eucharist in the Leabhar Breac affirms this teaching in very clear terms. It seems to echo the doctrine of the ninth-century German monk, Paschasius Radbertus. Throughout this lengthy work we come across strong affirmative statements such as: 'Although it be wheat and wine before the consecration, as is true, after the consecration it is the blood and fair, complete body.'[8]

We mentioned St Malachy at the beginning of this chapter. He was concerned not only with the correct carrying out of the liturgy but also, and more importantly, with the proper understanding and exposition of eucharistic faith. And so when he heard that a certain cleric of Lismore was apparently questioning the doctrine of the Real Presence, he decided to take action. He dealt humanely with the man, 'whose life was good but his faith not so'. He held a disputation with this cleric in the course of which his own well-reasoned argument in defence of Catholic orthodoxy prevailed.[9]

This concern with eucharistic faith was shared by another Irishman of roughly the same period, a monk by the name of Echtgus Úa Cúnáin of the community of Roscrea. It is possible that he is taking issue with this very same cleric of Lismore whose teaching was leading others astray. Here is an extract from his exposition on the Mass, written in verse form so that it might be more easily memorised and used in preaching by the clergy:

> The Son born of the Virgin, he it is thou consumest at the altar, nobly and completely, in the perfection of his body as blessed holy heaven contains it. May thy glorious faith and thy perfect belief be as follows: eat the body of the King in mysterious fashion in the form of an undiminished creature.[10]

Before the Reformation (thirteenth to sixteenth centuries)

This was no Golden Age for the Irish Church. In his book, *The Irish Catholic Experience*, Mgr Corish paints a bleak picture of the Church in this island during the period.[11] He speaks of grave abuses and of decay in ecclesiastical and monastic institutions. Of course it was a time of war, political upheaval and natural disasters such as the Black Death in the fourteenth century. Added to all that, there was friction between native Irish clergy and religious and their Norman/English associates. As a result of all these factors the pastoral care of the faithful suffered.

But there were positive influences at work as well. Here mention must be made of the contribution of the friars and other religious groups. In the course of the thirteenth century, Franciscans, Dominicans, Carmelites and Augustinians had come from England or the Continent and had settled in Ireland. If we single out the role of the Franciscan friars, it is on account of its exceptional impact.

The Franciscan contribution

Preaching of the Word of God was central to their mission. In his book, *The Friars Minor in Ireland*, Francis Cotter OFM describes how on Sundays and feast-days these men went from their friaries preaching the Word of God in parish churches and sometimes in a town square or even a field. They also preached in their own friary churches which had large naves to cater for the people rather than large sanctuaries for the clergy; for it was important that the congregation could see and hear the preacher.[12]

We get some idea of the kind of preaching the friars favoured from books surviving from this period, such as the *Liber exemplorum* and the Book of Multyfarnham (compiled in the second half of the thirteenth century). This latter contains sermons for the whole year corresponding to the order of readings used by the Roman curia. It was a rich resource for pastoral instruction. They preached about devotion to Christ crucified, the Blessed Virgin, and the importance of conversion. They also treated of the sacraments, especially Penance and the Eucharist.[13]

In preaching so insistently on the Eucharist, the friars were being faithful to the spirit and wishes of their founder. St Francis had a profound love of the Eucharist and directed his friars, especially during the latter years of his life, to encourage devotion to and reverence for the sacrament of Christ's Body and Blood. And so the friars helped to keep the faith alive and fostered a warm love of the Eucharist when religious life and practice were at a low ebb. This is in no way to underrate the contribution of the other religious orders such as the Dominicans, who also carried out an active ministry of preaching. It is significant, however, that the Franciscans underwent a profound reform in the fifteenth century. Coming at the eve of the Reformation, this reform was crucial for the maintenance of the Catholic faith. This 'Observant' reform, according to Corish, 'must have been by far the most powerful factor in lifting up the Christian mission'.[14]

Frequency of Communion
During the late medieval and pre-Reformation period, lay

people communicated rarely. It seems that, for the majority of them, sacramental Communion was limited to a few occasions in the year, such as Christmas, Easter and Pentecost. Indeed it may have been just once a year, at Easter, which was the minimum required by the Lateran Council of 1215. Such was the general practice throughout Europe. The situation in England in the fourteenth century is described by Eamonn Duffy in *The Stripping of the Altars*: 'For most people receiving Communion was an annual event . . . . In most parishes everyone went to Confession in Holy Week, and received Communion before or after High Mass on Easter Day.'[15] It is unlikely that the situation was very different in Ireland around this time.

It is difficult for us now to understand this strange reticence with regard to the sacrament. In the Catholic world today it is the normal practice, as it was in the early Church, for the faithful to communicate at the Mass in which they are participating. However, as noted in an earlier chapter, two Christian attitudes are legitimate: one is to accept the Lord's invitation, 'Take and eat, take and drink', while the other is to abstain out of a sense of unworthiness. We can identify either with the centurion who declared that he was not worthy, or with Zacchaeus who eagerly welcomed the Lord into his home. The people of medieval times identified more easily with the Roman centurion! And so, for a great proportion of the Christian faithful, seeing the Host during the elevation at Mass became a kind of substitute for sacramental Communion. It became a high point of lay experience of the Mass, and the notion of 'spiritual communion' to some extent compensated for the lack of sacramental encounter.

Returning now to Ireland, very sound advice on this matter is given by the monk of Roscrea already referred to:

> This sacrifice in an excellent manner has two sinless friends, officers of the King of heaven . . . . One of these has the custom of constantly and perpetually consuming it to heal his sins. And what, since he consumes it in a

holy manner could be better than this? The one who does not consume says this: 'In thy honour, King of heaven, I refrain. I am no worthy vessel; it is not unprofitable for me to say so.[16]

It is clear from this piece of advice that what is important is one's attitude and motivation. The Irish Church sought to strike the right balance. In a manuscript written at a Franciscan house in Co. Clare in the late fifteenth century, an anonymous friar tenders the following advice on 'the conditions for receiving the Body of Christ': '*Primo est tremendum in accipiendo, secundo est necessarium in sumendo, tercio est meritorium in credendo.*' We might render this in modern English as: 'It is awesome in taking, needful in receiving, meritorious in believing.'[17]

Looking ahead to a later century, it is interesting to find that the great Franciscan, Geoffrey Keating, in his treatise on the Mass written early in the seventeenth century, also emphasises the importance of proper dispositions and attitude. He declares that anyone whose love for God was growing daily could go to Mass and Communion every day, whereas one whose fear of God made him or her unworthy of Communion could refrain from receiving the sacrament of the Lord's body.[18]

The Reformation and after

On Easter Sunday 1551 the First Prayer Book of Edward VI was used in Christ Church Cathedral, Dublin, for the first time, in place of the Sarum liturgy.[19] The Reformation had arrived! On 11 January 1560 Parliament met in the same place and enacted both the Act of Supremacy (declaring the English monarch to be supreme head of the Irish as well as of the English Church), and the Act of Uniformity whereby the Book of Common Prayer replaced the Roman rite of Mass. By this latter Act, Irish Catholics were obliged to attend Protestant services on Sundays and Holy days. We now enter a period of repression and persecution that was to persist in varying degrees of severity for several centuries.

Of the long period following these enactments, Fr Edmond Cullinan writes: 'During the seventeenth to eighteenth centuries the public celebration of Catholic worship virtually disappeared because of legal repression. Such liturgy as there was took place in the countryside. It took place in private houses and in hidden places in the countryside.' He points out the positive side of this: 'The experience left the Irish people with a strong sense of the value of the Mass . . . it was recognised that the Eucharist was of central importance in the Christian life; people had risked their lives, and in some cases actually died, for their faithfulness to it.'[20]

Irish Catholics showed extraordinary tenacity in resisting the new laws. They were more successful than their counterparts in England who also held out against the changes. Sixteen years after the promulgation of the two Acts, Archbishop Loftus of Dublin had to confess the failure of the reform among the populace of Dublin. The same was true of other parts of the country; for example, complaints were made of 'Masses infinite in the city of Waterford'.

In his book, *Seventeen Irish Martyrs*,[21] Desmond Forristal gives graphic accounts of the trials of this varied group of people: 'one archbishop, three bishops, six priests, a religious brother, a widow, an alderman, a baker and three sailors'. In reading these accounts, one gets the unmistakable impression that the Mass was all-important to them. In fact it was this which kept them going. From the Eucharist they drew the strength of martyrdom. They could well have appropriated to themselves that Communion antiphon from the Antiphonary of Bangor: 'We have received the Body of Christ and we have drunk his blood; and so we will fear no evil, because the Lord is with us.'

In the context of the Mass and its celebration, some incidents from the accounts of the six priests are revealing. Take for example the story of Fr Maurice McKenraghty, chaplain to the Earl of Desmond. It was as he was about to begin the celebration of the Easter Mass in a private house in Clonmel in the year 1585 that he was interrupted by the soldiery and later arrested. He was hanged at Clonmel on 20 April 1585. The Franciscan priest, John Kearney, for nearly ten years carried out a daring apostolate in Ireland, somehow managing to evade detection. He achieved renown as a preacher, and he provided the people with Mass in secret places such as Mass-rocks. Finally he was arrested, tried, and condemned to death by hanging. His martyrdom took place in March 1653. The priestly ministry of the Augustinian, William Tirry, presents a marked contrast with that of Kearney. By natural inclination he was studious, reserved, prayerful. For three years he lived as a recluse in a small room devoting his time to reading, writing and praying. He ministered to those who came to seek his assistance. Arrested in 1654, and imprisoned at Clonmel, he turned his prison into a house of prayer. He was tried and sentenced to death, another martyr of the faith and 'hero of the Mass'. Such pastors really put heart into the people. Here we may recall the stirring words of Bishop Albert O'Brien of Limerick at the moment of his execution: 'Keep the faith, follow the commandments, seek nothing but the will of God.'

Recalling the memory of these martyrs should not be an occasion to reopen old sectarian wounds. We must bear in mind that throughout Europe during these centuries terrible deeds were committed in the name of religion by both Catholics and Protestants. Religious bigotry existed on both sides. Desmond Forristal shows considerable fair-mindedness in his book, as witness the following balanced assessment of the period: 'It was a period when little tolerance was shown on either side. There were Catholic governments in Europe who dealt ruthlessly with those who differed from them in religion. There were Protestant martyrs who chose to suffer and die rather than abandon their beliefs. Cruelty and bravery were to be found on either side of the religious divide.'[22]

Oliver Cromwell, who arrived in Ireland on 14 August 1649, regarded himself as a tolerant man, and, by the standards of the time, with some justification. A saying of his is much quoted: 'I meddle with no man's conscience.' It was no doubt sincerely meant at the moment it was spoken, and that was during his Irish campaign as he stood before the walls of New Ross parleying with its Governor, Sir Lucas Taafe, about terms of surrender. When asked about freedom of conscience for the people, he replied firmly: 'For that which you mention concerning liberty of conscience, I meddle with no man's conscience. But if by liberty of conscience you mean liberty to exercise the Mass, I judge it best to use plain dealing, and to let you know, where the Parliament of England have power, that will not be allowed of.'[23] The liberty he was prepared to grant was a very qualified one indeed. In excluding the Mass he struck at the heart of Catholic life and worship in Ireland.

In speaking of the martyrs we may not overlook St Oliver Plunkett (1629-81). He became Archbishop of Armagh in 1669. During the persecutions that began in 1673 he remained in Ireland, and, in the persecution following on the Titus Oates plot, he was taken prisoner, tried in London and executed for treason. He was the last Catholic to be martyred at Tyburn.[24]

Oliver Plunkett was a devoted lover of the Mass, and, in spite of persecution, sought to ensure that the sacred mysteries would be worthily celebrated throughout the country. At this point we may need to remind ourselves that the Mass rite in Ireland, as elsewhere at this time, was that of the Missal of Pius V, promulgated in 1570. This represented the so-called Tridentine Mass, the form of liturgy which continued for four hundred years in the Latin Church. This in turn was replaced in 1970 by a new Mass rite following the liturgical reforms of the Second Vatican Council. As Archbishop, Oliver Plunkett did all in his power to implement the decrees of the Council of Trent. He was very concerned about the training of priests and ordained a great number himself. In the Synod of Ardpatrick it was laid down that priests would be obliged to have 'at least one silver chalice to the value of fifty shillings with decent vestments, all of which should be left to the parish on the demise of the parish priest.'[25]

During his long captivity Oliver was denied the consolation of saying Mass. But a Benedictine fellow-prisoner, Dom

Maurus Corker, managed to procure for him a missal. With this he was able to 'satiate the ardent yearning of his heart by reading the Mass of the feast celebrated by the Church'. During the last week of his life on earth his longing to celebrate the Eucharist was satisfied. This was due to the help of some English Catholic friends who succeeded in bribing the gaoler to enable him to say the Mass in secret. He was thus strengthened and comforted by that 'divine pledge of present love and future glory'. He celebrated Mass for the last time at four in the morning on the day of his execution, 11 July 1681.

Penal times

These discriminatory laws were enacted by an all-Protestant parliament of 1697 in Dublin. While rarely enforced in all their severity, they weighed heavily on the Catholic community until they were finally repealed by the Act of Catholic Emancipation in 1829. But, as in the preceding century, the laws proved ineffective. Irish Catholics would not be coerced. In fact, according to Bishop McMahon of Clogher, writing about 1714: 'The greater the severity of the persecution, the greater the fervour of the people.'[26] It is the considered view of Mgr Patrick Corish that by the end of the eighteenth century Irish Catholics present the image of a Mass-going people.[27]

In popular imagination it is probably the Mass-rock which best symbolises the penal times in Ireland. These rocks are to be found in fields, woods or hills throughout the whole island. They provided the *mensa* (table) on which the Mass could be celebrated by a fugitive priest in a clandestine manner. While the local people prayed and offered the Mass with their priest, one of the congregation kept watch for fear of a raid by the soldiery.

Such a picture is by no means false even if it has been somewhat romanticised by writers of fiction. It represents the worst period of the penal times. It has been claimed that the period from 1650 to 1660 was in fact the darkest period of persecution. But even when the danger of arrest and imprisonment for clergy and their congregations had subsided, Mass-rocks continued to be in use either because the people

57

were too poor to build a Mass-house or because the local landlord refused to give land on which they could build one.

From the beginning of the eighteenth century both Mass-houses and Mass-rocks were in use. Mention of a 'Mass-house' should not suggest anything grandiose. A building of this kind generally amounted to little more than a thatched cabin open at one end. They were dark, cold and congested, but at least they offered some shelter from the wind and rain. For the poor people gathered around a Mass-rock there was no protection of any kind from the elements.

Mass-rocks are to be found throughout the four provinces. They are not so common in Leinster or Munster where Mass-houses were more numerous. They are plentiful in Connacht, not because of a stricter enforcement there of the penal code, but on account of the poverty of the people who had not the means to procure anything better. This was the situation to an even greater extent in Ulster where there were no Catholic landowners and where Catholics were confined to the poor land in the west of the province.[28]

Mass-rocks are often recognisable by the mark of one or more small crosses carved into the stone. The sites are generally known to the local people who take a legitimate pride in these monuments of their Christian past. People go to them as to holy wells, and, from time to time, Mass is celebrated at these sites. In a secluded glen in Glenstal there is a traditional Mass-rock which has been converted into a simple oratory. The Cistercian monasteries of Roscrea and Portglenone also possess one.

Fr Ó Laoghaire suggests that much work needs to be done on the old Mass-centres of pre-famine Ireland, and he points out the large number of place-names associated with Mass or including the word 'Aifreann'. The saying, 'it is the Mass that matters', which has become something of a cliché, is certainly true of the Ireland of that time. The people's conviction is admirably expressed in the Irish form: 'An tAifreann ná tugaigí ar aon phioc, níl ar bith sa saol níos fearr' (Abandon not the Mass for anything, nothing in the world surpasses it).[29]

58

After Catholic emancipation

After the granting of Catholic emancipation in 1829, the last of the discriminatory legislation was removed. For the Catholic Church in Ireland a new era had dawned. A phrase from the Song of Songs comes to mind: '*Iam hiems transiit*', 'the winter is over and gone'.

This was a period of rapid reconstruction. The re-establishment of public worship was already a reality, but now, in every parish, diocese and town, new churches were being built to replace the humble Mass-houses of penal times. The new edifices – parish churches, cathedrals, churches and chapels of religious orders – were of cut stone, richly ornate inside and designed mostly in the neo-Gothic style that was in favour at the time.

At this point we broach a rather controversial topic, namely the level of religious practice among the people in the early part of the nineteenth century. Much has been made by some historians and sociologists of a survey carried out in 1834 which sought to establish percentage figures for religious practice. The findings are rather surprising. With regard to attendance at Sunday Mass, the survey shows that the figures were high for the towns, somewhat lower for rural areas, and lowest of all in Irish-speaking regions. There the average attendance would have been 25% to 50%, according to Mgr Corish, correcting the American historian, David Miller, on this point.[30]

Statistics, especially of the rough sort carried out in the early decades of the last century, need careful assessment. In his interpretation of these findings Corish makes the important point that in the areas where religious practice appears to be lowest the people suffered the greatest disadvantages. They were very poor and deprived. The fact that many communities lacked even a rudimentary chapel meant that such liturgical services that they could avail of were not included in the survey.

The assumption that the people in Gaeltacht areas were less believing and less fervent is simply not tenable. There may indeed have been some decline in attendance at Sunday Mass in comparison with the preceding period, but, in general, the people of Gaelic-speaking Connacht and Ulster were not less devout than their compatriots elsewhere. Quite the contrary in fact, as scholars like Bishop Joseph Duffy and others are ready to demonstrate. Fr Diarmuid Ó Laoghaire takes issue with Miller on this point. He also repudiates the claim of Emmet Larkin, in an article written in *The American Historical Review* (1972), that 'most of the two million Irish who emigrated between 1847 and 1860 were part of the generation of non-practising Catholics, if indeed they were Catholics at all'.[31] He wonders if such a generalisation could be made by someone who had read and studied Irish-language sources such as Douglas Hyde's *The Religious Songs of Connacht*. This rich treasury of folk-prayers bears eloquent testimony to the religious faith of the people, and in particular to their love of the Mass and the Lord's Day. In the next chapter we will consider these 'paidreacha' which have sprung spontaneously from the heart of a people.

Turning now to the second half of the nineteenth century, we can observe an extraordinary expansion of Catholic life in Ireland. Here the phrase 'devotional revolution', coined by Larkin, is appropriate. It is a period very much associated with one dominant ecclesiastical figure, Cardinal Paul Cullen, Archbishop of Armagh from 1849 to 1852, and Archbishop of Dublin from 1852 to 1878. Due to his personal initiative and active campaigning there resulted a great increase in sacramental practice, especially with regard to Confession and the Mass. He also introduced and popularised eucharistic devotions outside of Mass such as Benediction of the Blessed Sacrament.[32]

Paul Cullen had spent many years in Rome and was a great devotee of everything Roman. He favoured Italian-style devotions, and introduced them to this country. He does not seem to have been deeply aware of the riches inherent in traditional Irish spirituality. In his interesting book, *Irish Catholics, Tradition and Transition* (Dublin: Veritas, 1980), Fr John Ó Ríordáin CSSR, is very critical of this tendency on the part of Cullen and other churchmen to Romanise all aspects of Irish Catholic life. It is unfortunate that this was the case, and at a time when the Irish language was in sharp decline in rural Ireland. On the other hand, we must give the Cardinal credit for his very positive achievements. During his long period of spiritual leadership attendance at Sunday Mass increased rapidly, reaching close on a hundred per cent by the end of the century. New churches were not only built but carefully maintained. From this time onwards the Blessed Sacrament was always kept in the church with a lamp burning before it.

The Station Mass

The practice of having Mass said in people's homes goes back to penal times. Towards the end of this period and throughout the nineteenth century, the custom took on the form of the 'Station Mass'. This was a very interesting development, and peculiarly Irish. The arrangement was roughly as follows. In each parish or townland certain houses were designated for the Stations. Generally the Stations took place twice a year, before Christmas and Easter. The purpose was to prepare the people for these great festivals by providing them with Confession and Mass in their homes. Obviously the Mass was not confined to the family of the household: the neighbours were invited as well. It also was an opportunity for the visiting priest to bring Holy Communion to the homes of the old and infirm who were unable to come even to the Stations.[33]

At the Synod of Thurles in 1850, the practice was called into question, mainly by Cardinal Cullen, on the ground of alleged abuses. Archbishop Slattery of Cashel strongly supported the custom and was able to ensure that the usage of Mass Stations was recognised by ecclesiastical law. He was convinced of the pastoral value of the time-honoured and very popular custom. And so the Stations continued in the Cashel diocese and, indeed, throughout the whole country with the exception of Dublin. At a Synod in 1853 the practice was virtually excluded from the Dublin province except for the more remote rural areas. But even in these out-of-the-way places, the policy was to move the Stations from homes to the parish church. The people of the area would come to the church on a particular day for their Station Mass. This latter practice was later adopted elsewhere in Ireland.

It was a great privilege to have one's house chosen for a Station Mass. Weeks of cleaning and painting went into preparing for the great day which was both a social as well as a religious occasion. Vivid accounts of these Stations are to be found in literature, both historical and fictional. Among the examples that come to mind are some accounts in the novels of Canon Sheehan. There is the description of the Station Mass at Glencarn in *My New Curate*. Then we have a moving account of a Mass said in the bedroom of a poor, sightless woman in *The Blindness of Dr Gray*. For our own time we have two charming and nostalgic accounts of 'the Stations' in Alice Taylor's book of reminiscences, *To School through the Fields* (Dingle: Brandon, 1988). One chapter bears the title, 'Preparing for the Stations', and another 'Beneath God's Altar'. The latter describes the Mass in the home of an eccentric old lady who was none too tidy. The kindly parish priest and his curate acceded to her request to have a Station all for herself. Young Alice was the only other person invited. There is that touching moment, just before his departure, when the parish priest turns to the child and says: 'Little girl, God is found in strange places. Try not to forget this morning.' The tradition of the Station Mass never entirely died out, although by the middle of this century it was in severe decline and had disappeared in many parts. It was given a new lease of life as a result of the liturgical reforms of the Second Vatican Council. Side by side with the parochial Mass bringing together the local church, the need was felt for occasional eucharistic celebrations in a more intimate setting such as the home or school. This is well explained in that excellent booklet, *The Small-Group Mass*, published in the 1970s by the Dublin Diocesan Liturgical Commission.

The road to the Second Vatican Council

The complete restoration of Catholic life and religious practice in Ireland is perhaps best symbolised by the Eucharistic Congress held at Dublin in 1932. The memory of that event still lives on in folk memory. The undisputed high point of the days of celebration was the great open-air Mass held at the Phoenix Park in the presence of close on a million people. The most poignant moment in that celebration, one that recalled centuries of faith and fidelity, was the ringing of the bell of St Patrick during the Consecration. Another unforgettable experience of the Congress was the ceremony of Benediction of the Blessed Sacrament held on O'Connell Bridge. An uncle of my own, now dead, recalls the impression made on the vast crowd by the singing of *Panis angelicus* by the great Irish tenor John McCormack. Ireland was celebrating, on the occasion of this congress, the nation's fifteen-hundredth anniversary of its conversion to Christianity. Under the circumstances, some degree of 'triumphalism' was surely legitimate. . .

That Irish Catholics in the first half of this century were overwhelmingly a Mass-going people is an undisputed fact of history, however one may question their motives. But we must bear in mind that it was an all-Latin Mass with little active involvement on the part of the laity. Apart from the few who possessed vernacular missals, there was little understanding of the prayers and readings. No doubt many devout Mass-goers were reasonably satisfied with this state of affairs and used the time of worship to get on with their own private prayers and devotions. From this form of celebration came the expression, 'the blessed murmur of the Mass' (referring to the priest's semi-inaudible recitation of the Eucharistic Prayer) was coined. The normal form of celebration was a silent 'Low Mass', at which the presbyter said almost everything and the people 'assisted'. At a deep, interior level, they could and did participate intensely, but there was little external expression of this apart from the reception of Holy Communion which, thanks to the encouragement of Pope St Pius X (1835-1914), was now much more frequent.

But winds of change were blowing in the Church. In France, Belgium, Germany, and later in the United States, the liturgical movement was gathering momentum. The great goal of this movement was to achieve the 'full and active participation' of the people in the liturgy. What activated the promoters of this new movement was the realisation that the Church, the People of God, is a 'priestly people'. By very reason of their baptism the Christian faithful are 'deputed to worship', and so have the privilege and right to share in a full, active and conscious way in the eucharistic sacrifice. The so-called 'dialogue Mass' was a first attempt at involving the laity in the celebration of the Mass. But as time went on, the need for a vernacular liturgy became more keenly felt. New ideas, even when they express forgotten truths, will invariably encounter opposition, and Church leaders tend to be particularly wary of proposed changes in liturgy. For that reason, the pioneers of the movement were greatly encouraged when, in 1947, Pope Pius XII issued his encyclical, *Mediator Dei*, which was regarded as an endorsement of the main principles and aspirations of the liturgical movement.

Here in Ireland the liturgical movement was a rather late starter although there was no lack of priests and religious imbued with a deep love of the liturgy and a strong pastoral sense. The late Dr J.G. McGarry of Maynooth, himself a keen promoter of pastoral liturgy, writing in *Liturgical Arts* (August 1961), made the following shrewd observation: 'As a movement of extrinsic origin, the liturgical movement seems to our countrymen too little concerned about essential matters, too little in key with Irish piety, with its personal, eucharistic and ascetic ethos.'[34]

It could be said that the liturgical movement in Ireland began with liturgical music, and much was done to promote the use of Gregorian chant as a form of congregational prayer. Many schools of boys and girls participated in musical festivals ('feiseanna') in which competitions were held for the best choir performances of plain chant. Among the pioneers of this movement were Fr John Burke of Dublin, and Fr Winoc

Mertens of Glenstal. It is greatly to be regretted that all this hard-won competence in traditional liturgical chant was not put to greater use in our parishes.

The annual Glenstal Liturgical Congress, beginning in 1954, provided a forum where new ideas could be discussed and evaluated. Here the best of European scholarship met in creative dialogue with Irish pastoral experience. Irish priests had the opportunity to hear scholars such as Fr Josef Jungmann SJ and Dr Balthasar Fischer who were not only pioneers of the liturgical movement in their own countries, but were later to play a significant role in the implementation of the Liturgy Constitution, *Sacrosanctum Concilium*, of the Second Vatican Council.

With the Council, and the liturgical reforms emanating from it, we have reached a new stage in the history of the Mass in Ireland. Again and again we must go back to a cardinal principle of the conciliar document: 'In the restoration and promotion of the sacred liturgy, the full and active participation of the people is the aim to be considered before all else' (CSL, 14). More than thirty years on, that *plena et actuosa participatio* has assuredly not yet been fully achieved, but we have certainly moved towards a more participative and congregational-type liturgy with a wider distribution of roles. Irish Catholics accepted the liturgical reforms of the Council with good grace, if not great enthusiasm. We have been spared the worst effects of that polarisation between conservatives and progressives which manifested itself in other countries. Only a tiny minority of enthusiasts favour a return to the Latin Tridentine Mass.

The post-conciliar period would require a chapter in itself, but we must draw our survey to a close. The ensuing decades have been ones of unprecedented change in the social, economic and cultural spheres. For the Church in this country it has been both 'the best of times and the worst of times'. As an institution and in its leadership it has been challenged as never before, the penal times included. And yet in spite of a worrying downward trend in the religious practice of the younger age groups, the Eucharist continues to hold a central place in the faith life of our people. The seeds of liturgical reform have been planted in the good and generous soil of a nation's faith. It is for us pastors to ensure that the ripe fruit will not be delayed. We must do our part and leave the rest to God. The renewal must continue: the liturgy, like the Church itself, is ever in need of reform, *semper reformanda*. Where this reform is concerned, the words of Pope Paul VI still hold true: 'Everything has been said, everything still remains to be done.' Whatever form the eucharistic celebration may take, it will continue to be 'the Mass we always knew'. 'It is the Mass that matters', it used to be said. May the Mass continue to matter to our people, and intensely so.

5
sunday prayers of the people

In this chapter we will consider the rich heritage of prayers that has its source in the religious sentiment of our people. These belong to the oral tradition of the Gaeltacht areas of Munster, Connacht and Ulster. They celebrate in word and song the coming of Sunday as a day of festive joy and of sacramental encounter with Christ who is welcomed as 'Rí an Domhnaigh', 'King of Sunday'. They constitute an impressive witness to popular devotion to the Mass.

These prayers were widely used and take many forms. Throughout the Irish-speaking areas of our land these fervent and easily-remembered prayers were spoken by the people at home, on their way to Mass, in the church, before and after Communion, and on their way home. They were also added to the Rosary prayer. With the decline of the Irish language they are perhaps less known and valued in modern times than in the past. Happily a revival now seems to be taking place as popular editions of the prayers are made available in both Irish and English.

These and other similar Gaelic folk-prayers were collected and published at the beginning of this century by scholars such as Douglas Hyde in his *Religious Songs of Connacht*, and Úna Ní Ógáin in her smaller compilation, *Dánta Dé* (Religious Poems). In recent years Fr Diarmuid Ó Laoghaire SJ has made available that wonderful collection of over five hundred prayers and blessings in *Ár bPaidreacha Dúchais* (Our Native Prayers). A selection of the latter, in Irish and a free verse-rendering in English, has recently appeared as *Prayers of Two Peoples*, the work of Fr Stephen Redmond SJ.[1]

Here is one version of a very popular Sunday prayer. It is taken from the collection, *Saltair – Urnaithe Dúchais* (Prayers from the Irish Tradition), edited by Pádraig Ó Fiannachta and Desmond Forristal (Dublin, Columba Press, 1988, pp. 24-25):

Dé bheatha chugainn, a Dhomnaigh bheannaithe,
(We bid you welcome, blessed Sunday)
Lá breá aoibhinn tar éis na seachtaine,
(A fine lovely day after the week)
Lá breá aoibhinn chun Críost a agallamh.
(A fine and lovely day to speak to Christ.)
Corraigh do chos is téire chun an Aifrinn.
(Stir you feet and make your way to Mass.)
Corraigh do chroí agus díbir an ghangaid as.
(Stir your heart and drive from it all spite.)
Corraigh do bhéal chun bréithre beannaithe.
(Stir your lips and speak words of blessing.)
Féach suas ar Mhac na Banaltran,
(Look up and see the Son of the blessed Nurse,)
Mac na hÓige, ós é cheannaigh sinn,
(the Son of the Virgin, for it was he who redeemed us;)
Gur leis a bhuafar beo agus marbh sinn.
(may we be his in life and in death.)

What follows is a reflective commentary on this short prayer. By comparing it with similar prayer-forms in the Irish language, we attempt to uncover the rich depths of meaning it contains.

Welcoming Sunday
The prayer begins with a welcoming 'Dé bheatha chugainn' to Sunday. In many forms of the prayer the greeting is the familiar 'Fáilte' ('Welcome'). Sunday is welcomed as a friend coming to the house. How interesting that the Christian Sabbath is personified in this way! The only similar form of address in the liturgy occurs in that beautiful Easter hymn, '*Salva festa dies*', ('Hail festive day'). Is not Sunday a weekly Easter, and is not Easter 'the great Sunday', 'An Domhnach Mór', as it is known in Irish?

So Sunday, unlike the other days of the week, takes on a personality of its own. This trait of the Irish folk prayers has been studied by the German priest-scholar, Balthasar Fischer of Trier. Conversant with the folk traditions of other European countries, Dr Fischer concludes that this particular Irish characteristic is almost unique. In Christian tradition, the nearest parallel is be found in Ethiopic liturgical piety where Sunday is personified, greeted and bidden farewell like a beloved guest. Surprisingly, an even closer parallel is discernible in Jewish spirituality. Here the Sabbath is also personified: it is greeted, welcomed and celebrated as a queen. On Friday evening in every home a candle is lit to welcome in the Seventh Day. The privilege of lighting the candle and saying the accompanying prayer of blessing belongs to the woman of the house. As in the home so in the synagogue there occurs the ceremony of welcoming in the 'Sabbath Queen'. On the conclusion of the day of rest and worship, a little ceremony of 'farewell to the Sabbath' takes place.[2]

In the *Veritas Book of Blessing Prayers* (Dublin, 1989, p. 126), there is found a beautiful blessing for the 'Start of the Lord's Day'. It is inspired by the Jewish custom of lighting the Sabbath candle in the home on the eve of the holy day. At the start of the Saturday evening meal or at another suitable time, one person may light a candle as a sign of welcoming the Lord's Day. Another person prays the following or a similar prayer:

> Blessed are you, O Lord our God, our Father, King of the universe:
> You created light in order to scatter the darkness of our lives.
> You fill us with the Spirit of Jesus so that we may live by his light.
> We bless your holy name as we kindle this light, one of your many gifts to us.
> Rekindle, we pray, the flame of the Holy Spirit as we praise you for this day of the Lord.

The King of Sunday

In many of the native Irish prayers, including the Sunday prayer, we find the expression, 'Rí an Domhnaigh', 'The King of Sunday'. Here are some forms of address using this title: 'Fáilte romhat (or céad fáilte) romhat, a Rí an Domhnaigh', 'Welcome (or a hundred welcomes) to you, King of the Sunday'. One of the Sunday prayers begins with the greeting: 'Céad fáilte romhat, a Rí an Domhnaigh bheannaithe', 'A thousand welcomes to you, King of blessed Sunday'.

This word, 'Rí' (King), is obviously a favourite form of address. Christ is addressed as King of creation, of the stars, of the days of the week, and especially of those two days sanctified by the Passion and Resurrection of Christ, Friday and Sunday. But it is especially the appellation, 'Rí an Domhnaigh', 'King of Sunday', that keeps recurring.

What is its significance? In an Irish context the term is both reverential and intimate. It may be said that, at a theological level, the term 'Rí' is equivalent to the biblical *Kurios* ('Lord'). By his victory over the forces of evil, Jesus was constituted Lord and Saviour. So the term 'King' here expresses faith and reverence. But the king in question is not a remote, detached monarch. He is very close to his people. In a land of innumerable petty kingdoms, the local 'Rí' was familiar to all his subjects. They knew him and he knew them in an intimate and personal way. And so the people's attitude to their king was one of profound respect and homage, but also one of kinship and familiarity. Is not this the relationship that should exist between Christ and his people? In this relationship, both transcendence and intimacy have their place. Christ is both 'High King of heaven' and 'King of my heart'.[3]

A fine holiday

We return now to our prayer and consider the expression, 'lá breá aoibhinn tar éis na seachtaine', 'a fine and lovely day after the week'. For our people Sunday is both a holy day and a holiday, a day of rest from their labours, of joy and relaxation, as well as of prayer and worship. The day was looked forward to with eager expectation, and relished when it came.

Sunday is acclaimed as 'cinn óir na seachtaine', 'the golden head of the week', and 'crown of all the seven days'. We also find the expression, 'A Dhomnaigh gléigeal', 'O pure bright Sunday'. There is a folk-tale of a man who, in carrying out some tasks assigned to him, finds a bird's nest which has one golden and six silver eggs in it. It is later explained to him that the golden egg represents Sunday, the silver ones the other days of the week.[4]

Meeting with Christ

'Lá breá aoibhinn chun Críost a agallamh', 'a full lovely day to speak to Christ'. What a beautiful description of Sunday! Sunday is the Lord's Day, which means that every moment of it belongs to him. It is the day of the covenant, the day of meeting with Christ in the Eucharist. This does not mean that there is no place for leisure activities, for sport and entertainment, but it does mean putting first things first, and in our order of priorities prayer and worship of the Lord must come first.

'A full lovely day to speak to Christ.' One is reminded of St Teresa's description of prayer as a 'loving conversation with him by whom we know that we are loved'. Another form of the prayer has the words: 'Lá agus oíche chun Críost a fhreagairt', 'A day and a night for answering Christ'. This reinforces the notion of prayer as a dialogue, a colloquy, a loving exchange, and this takes place at a personal as well as a community level on Sunday. It is a day we consecrate to the Lord by prayer and works of love.

The walk to Mass

'Corraigh do chos is téire chun an Aifrinn', 'Stir your feet and make your way to Mass'. This line expresses the eagerness and sense of purpose with which people set out for Mass on a Sunday morning. The Mass was the goal and crown of the Sunday celebration.

The walk to Mass was very important. Even in our own

time I have heard of old people who preferred to walk to church rather than accept a lift; it was their way of paying homage to the Lord of the Sabbath. The cover illustration of this book is taken from that fine painting by James Humbert Craig called, 'Walking to Mass', which is to be seen in the Crawford Gallery, Cork. The scene is in Connemara, the region clearly recognisable by its small fields and low stone walls. A long line of local people is wending its way to the church. Here and there a bicycle or pony and trap is to be seen, but most of the Mass-goers are making their way on foot.

A correspondent to *The Furrow*, Turlough Breatnach, has commented on that painting by Craig.[5] He suggests that there is something highly significant in the walk. It represents the People of God, always a people on the march. It conjures up the desert journey to the Promised Land under the leadership of Moses and Joshua. It also suggests walks in the New Testament: Jesus with his disciples walking through Palestine, his walk to Emmaus with the two disciples. It reminds us of his call, 'Come, follow me', and the challenge to take up our cross and go the whole way with him to Calvary. St Paul's missionary journeys also come to mind. Finally, in every age and place, the Church is the People of God *en route* to the heavenly city, the New Jerusalem.

From this viewpoint, the walk to Mass has a kind of liturgical character: it can be likened to a procession. It is part of the preparation for Mass, and we know that along the way the beautiful 'Welcome to Sunday' prayer, and prayers on seeing the church were said. At the ordinary human level the walk was also an occasion to express friendship and neighbourliness as individuals and family groups met along the way.

Worship of the heart

We now consider lines four and five of the prayer which show that Christianity is not just a matter of external observance but is essentially a religion of the heart. Jesus reminds us that mercy is worth more than sacrifice, and that we must honour the Father not only with our lips but also, and more importantly, with our hearts. He taught his disciples that if they have a gift to offer at the altar and there remember that their brother has something against them, they must leave their gift before the altar, go and be reconciled with their brother and then come back and offer their gift (Matthew 5:23).

It is in this Gospel spirit that we read the lines: 'Corraigh do chroí agus díbir an ghangaid as', 'Stir your heart and drive out all spite', and 'Corraigh do bhéal chun bréithre beannaithe', 'Stir your lips and speak words of blessing'.

The word 'ghangaid' is a strong one, connoting venom, spite, that evil root of bitterness which acts as a cancer and can corrode a community. 'Pray for those who persecute you', says Christ; 'If you are cursed, answer with a blessing', says Paul. In this prayer we not only stifle feelings of ill will, but positively seek the good of even those who have done us harm. The Christian who is maligned must not repay in kind but answer with a blessing. The Irish language is full of these 'briathra beannaithe', 'words of blessing'.

Even today, in both vernaculars, Irish people, especially in rural areas, make frequent use of blessings. There are blessings for all times and occasions. In *Ár bPaidreacha Dúchais*, Fr Diarmuid Ó Laoghaire provides a wide range of traditional blessings – of God, of people, of animals and of inanimate things. There is one which is truly universal in character. It is titled 'Beannacht ar chách' ('Blessing on everyone'):

> *Nára tiugha féar ag fás*
> (Not more numerous the growing blades of grass)
> *Ná gaineamh ar thrá*
> (Nor the grains of sand on the shore)
> *Ná drúcht ar bhán*
> (Nor the dewdrops on the pasture)
> *Ná na beannachtaí ó Rí na ngrást*
> (be the blessings of the King of graces)
> *le gach anam a bhí, a bheidh nó 'tá.*
> (on every soul that was, that will be or that is.)

73

Mary, our Nurse-Mother

'Féach suas ar Mhac na Banaltran', 'Look up and see the Son of the Blessed Nurse'. It is Christ, not Mary or any saint, who is the Saviour. To look up at him – on the cross, in glory – with faith and longing, is to be saved. But Christ is never separated from his mother. The lives and mysteries of Mother and Son are inseparably interwoven. Irish spirituality is strong on this association. So often we meet the expression 'Son of Mary', or 'Son of the Virgin'. How frequently in the 'paidreacha' is Mary's name included in prayers to Christ?

At first, this use of the word 'nurse' may seem rather strange. In itself 'banaltra' is not a mystical term, it can apply to almost any kind of nurse. But I believe it expresses very well the human, maternal role of Mary. It corrects the impression, suggested by a certain kind of art, that Mary was an aristocratic lady who would in all likelihood have left the nursing of her baby to others. On the contrary, she was fully involved in all the very demanding, physical aspects of mothering. Mary is thus a very human person with whom everyone, in particular every mother, can readily identify. This use of the term 'banaltra' is by no means unique, we meet it in a similar context in other prayers. In the collection *Threshold of Light* (ed. Allchin/E. de Waal), there is included a poem-prayer to Mary where we find the tender term of address : 'Calm Nurse-Mother of Christ'.

But Mary is a Virgin Mother, and Christ is 'Mac na hÓige', 'Son of the Virgin'. It is he who 'bought us' ('a cheannaigh sinn'), who rose from the dead, who redeemed us by his glorious Death and Resurrection. He is not only the universal Saviour but the personal Saviour of each one. And so the prayer, with its delicate allusion to Mary, is strongly Christ-centred and rooted in the dogma of the redemption.

Self-offering

'Gur leis a bhuafar beo agus marbh sinn', 'May we be his in life and in death'.

This strikes a deeply spiritual note, and recalls a Pauline

passage: 'For none of us lives to himself, and none of us dies to himself; while we are alive, we are living for the Lord, and when we die, we die for the Lord: and so, alive or dead, we belong to the Lord' (Rm 14:7). We belong to Christ by Baptism, but the handing over of ourselves to him must be re-affirmed time and again throughout life; and what more suitable occasion than the Lord's Day and in the course of the Mass!

Other forms of the Sunday prayer present extended versions of this theme. Thus, 'Cuirim m'anam ort, a Dhia, is ní raghaidh mé ina dhiadh go bráth', 'I enjoin my soul on you, O God, and I will not make a claim on it for ever'. Here is a profound and truly authentic note of Irish spirituality. It expresses a sentiment that has its source in the activity of 'conversing' with Christ. True prayer leads to generous self-offering.

This self-offering can be made to the Father in union with Christ or directly to Christ. Several prayers in Ó Laoghaire's collection take the latter form, and it is significant that they occur within the context of the Mass. Thus, 'Bronnaim m'anam ort, a Íosa Críost, ní iarrfad ort é choíche ná go brách', 'I offer my soul to you, King of the graces, and I will never ask you for it back'.[6] This is part of a prayer said before Mass. The following is said in preparation for the Gospel: 'Bronnaim m'anam duitse, a Rí na ngrásta, agus go brách nár lige tú mé ar ais', 'I offer my soul to you, King of graces, never allow me to take it back'.[7] There is a similar prayer after Communion: 'Toirbhrim duitse mé féin, a Chríost, nár scara mé leat a choích arís', 'I offer (dedicate) myself to you, O Christ, never allow me to be separated from you again'.[8] Finally, the following act of self-offering is said on leaving the church: 'Fillim ar Mhuire agus casaim ar Íosa, bronnaim suas m'anam go bhfeicfead sibh arís', 'I bow to Mary and I turn to Jesus; I offer up my soul now and always, and I will continue to offer it until I see you both again'.[9]

The attitude of constant attention and total submission to God is characteristic of the Celtic saints. This is borne out by the following little story about St Brendan and St Brigid:

> It is told of St Brendan that he asked one day of St
> Brigid how was the love of God with her, and that she
> asked him to speak for himself first, and he confessed
> that since he took orders he had never gone over seven
> ridges without having his mind on God. After which
> Brigid said: by the Virgin's Son, that from the time she
> had set her mind on God she had never taken it back
> from him.[10]

This was not just the attitude of great saints, it also
characterised the spiritual outlook of a very great number of
layfolk as well. These lived constantly in the awareness of
God's presence, and, in good days as well as in bad, could
accept the divine plan with a cheerful 'Fáilte roimh thoil Dé',
'Welcome to the will of God'.

Prayers during Mass
Apart from the great Sunday prayer that we have been
considering, there are many other prayers and exclamations
said during the Mass which welcome Christ sacramentally
present. A wide selection is given in *Ár bPaidreacha Dúchais*.
Thus, after the consecration: 'Céad míle fáilte, a Thiarna', 'A
hundred thousand welcomes to you, O Lord'; 'Fáilte romhat,
a Shlánitheoir', 'Welcome to you, O Saviour'; 'Céad míle fáilte
romhat, a Rí an Domhnaigh', 'A hundred thousand welcomes
to you, King of Sunday'.

There are other fervent exclamations and prayers said after
Communion, and they are also in the welcoming mode. Here
is an example: 'Míle fáilte romhat, a Choirp an Tiarna, tá tú
agam anois; glan an áit 'na bhfuilir, díbir rúta an pheaca; is a
Mhaighdean glórmhar, tar i m' choimhdeacht', 'A thousand
welcomes to you, Body of Christ, you are in my possession
now; cleanse the place where you find yourself, expel the roots
of sin; and you, glorious Virgin, come as my companion'.

Here is another Communion prayer welcoming the
Saviour. It is number 117 in *Ár bPaidreacha Dúchais*:

Fáilte mharthanach mhúinte romhat, a Thiarna,
(A lasting, gracious welcome to you, O Lord)
    fáilte mar an taoile romhat,
(a welcome like the tide to you)
    fáilte an athar roimh leanbh atá i mbroinn go fóill romhat,
(a welcome like that of father to the child still in the womb to
    you)
    fanacht gan imeacht ach fanacht linn féin go deo romhat.
(We bid you stay without departing, but to stay with us
    always.)

The rough translation is my own, but the spirit of the prayer is
so much better conveyed in Stephen Redmond's free
rendering:

    I welcome you in love and courtesy
    my welcome's like a torrent, full and free
    like a father's for his infant in the womb
    stay, Lord – in my heart there's always room.[11]

Here is a prayer that evokes the blood and water that flowed
from the side of Christ:[12]

    Míle fáilte romhat, 'Íosa uasail, a Thiarna,
(A thousand welcomes to you, noble Jesus, Lord)
    a d'fhulaing dúinne an Pháis,
(who endured the Passion for us)
    an tsleá nimhe a dhul trí do thaobh
(whose side was pierced by the poisoned spear)
    gur tháinig as fuil agus uisce,
(until there came out of it blood and water),
    'Íosa, Mac Muire, déan trócaire orainn.
(O Jesus, Son of Mary, have mercy on us.)

The healing Christ
In time of illness Christ is also invoked as 'Rí an Domhnaigh'.

A fine example of such a prayer comes from an Anglo-Norman poet of the fifteenth century, Richard Butler. The poem is quoted by John Ó Ríordáin in *Irish Catholics*, where he also gives a translation:[13]

> *Rí an Domhnaigh mo dhoctúir-si*
> (May the King of Sunday, my doctor)
> *is Muire liaigh dom leighis*
> (And Mary, my physician in my illness)
> *'s a chroch neamh gan róthuirsi*
> (and the holy cross – grant, that without too great sorrow)
> *go sgaraid mhé rem theinnis.*
> (I shall be parted from my illness.)

Similar faith in the healing power of Christ, as well as in the intercession of Mary, is expressed in a prayer-poem of later times composed by the Gaelic poet, Tomás Rua Ó Súilleabháin, a native of Iveragh, Co. Kerry. As he lay very ill in a Dublin fever hospital, homesick and in pain, he poured out his feelings in a long, poignant poem which seeks healing both of his bodily and spiritual ills.

The poem begins with an invocation to the King of Sunday: 'A Rí an Domhnaigh, thar le cabhair chugham, is tóg i n-am ó 'n bpéin mé' ('King of Sunday, come to my aid, and deliver me soon from my pain'). But Christ is not only King of Sunday, he is Lord of all the days. And so the poet proceeds to address him in the following stanzas as King also of Monday, Tuesday, Wednesday, and so through the whole week. With firm faith in the healing power of Christ, the poet earnestly asks for the restoration of his health, for remission of his past transgressions and for deliverance on the Day of Judgment.

Like the earlier poet, Tomás Rua also turns to Mary, and through her intercession, seeks healing from her as well. Then he invokes too the prayers of St Brigid who, because she resembled so closely the Mother of Jesus in her faith and obedience to the will of God, was known as 'Mary of the Gael'.

This deeply spiritual poem has been set to music by the late Seán Ó Riada. A shortened version of this setting is to be found in the *Veritas Hymnal* (no. 50, p. 42). Nóirín Ní Riain also includes the poem with music in *A Wealth of Songs from the Irish Tradition* (Cork, Mercier Press, 1988, p. 28). She provides two authentic sung versions in her thesis, *The Music of Traditional Religious song in Irish* (see pp. 78 and 97).

In two languages

The Sunday prayers, once so popular among Gaelic-speaking people, are too little-known among the general populace. One of the reasons is surely the scarcity of popular translations. Scholars readily admit that it is peculiarly difficult to convey in a natural-sounding English the rhythm, imagery and word patterns of the Gaelic.

Difficult, but by no means impossible! An excellent version of the Sunday prayer by Douglas Hyde is found in his *The Religious Songs of Connacht* (Irish University Press, 1972, p. 381). It is simple and robust. In his *Prayers of two Peoples* (p. 29), Fr Stephen Redmond also adopts the verse form, and is eminently successful in transposing to English the simple beauty and vital spirit of the original:

> Welcome, blessed Sunday!
> crown of all the seven days
> day of God, of meeting Christ
> of thanks and praise.
>
> Turn your feet to go to Mass
> start to say the blessed word
> throw away the chains of sin
> look to the Lord.
>
> Face that's brighter than the sun
> do not keep me on the rack
> Lord, receive my heart and soul
> no asking back.

6
at prayer and at play

'The day of the Lord, O day of joy, blessed day, venerable day, on which the people come together to the Church!' This joyful exclamation, which comes from a late ninth- or early tenth-century Celtic source, seems an appropriate opening to this chapter.[1] Here we will treat of the Sabbath rest, of prayer and worship, and also of the family, social and recreational aspects of Sunday. It was never intended to be a dour or dull day; rather it is the day of which the psalmist exclaims: 'This is the day which the Lord has made, let us rejoice and be glad in it.' Even the stern Irish penitentials of long ago strictly forbade fasting or other forms of penance on the Lord's Day.[2] And, as we have noted in the previous chapter, our people welcomed Sunday as 'lá breá saoire', 'a fine holiday', a truly festive day.

Since the Second Vatican Council, Church legislation concerning the Lord's Day is notably positive and liberating: the faithful are to observe Sunday as 'a day of joy and freedom from work' (Liturgy Constitution, 106). In a similar vein, the revised Code of Canon Law declares: 'On Sunday and other holy days of obligation the faithful are obliged to participate in the Mass. They are also to abstain from such work or business that would inhibit the worship to be given to God, the joy proper to the Lord's Day, or the due relaxation of mind and body' (can. 1247). In a fine section on the Christian Sabbath, the Catechism of the Catholic Church declares: 'The institution of the Lord's Day helps everyone enjoy adequate rest and leisure to cultivate their familial, cultural, social and religious lives' (2184).

It is true that in the not too distant past regulations

concerning Sunday observance were rather restrictive. The Sabbath rest was taken seriously, and all forms of 'unnecessary servile work' were strictly forbidden. It is said that the poet Clarence Mangan (1803-49) refused to accept payment for work he was obliged to do in a scrivener's office on Sunday. Nearer our own time, Phil O'Keefe describes in her book, *Down Cobbled Streets*, how a Catholic family spent Sunday in the Dublin of the 1930s.[3] All observe the Sabbath rest: no knitting or sewing or washing of clothes, no clipping of the hedge or digging in the garden. The day always started with Mass at which everyone wore their 'Sunday best'. In the afternoon the children always took a walk with their mother through the streets or along the river or to the Phoenix Park. All business premises and trading outlets were closed.

Properly understood, the observance of Sunday as a non-working day is not a curtailment of human freedom. On the contrary, the purpose of the legislation is positive and liberating. The biblical Sabbath liberated slaves from their hard physical toil to enable them to share in the physical and spiritual rest of their people and to engage in the worship of their God. For the Church too, when legislation was first introduced, the concern was for the welfare of the most deprived of its members. The prohibition was not directed against servile work as such, rather, the intention was to enable slaves and farm-labourers to rest on the Lord's Day and so to free them for worship.[4] Turning to an Irish source, the *Letter of Jesus on Sunday Observance* gives as reason why it is wrong for masters to deny their subjects rest from work on Sunday: 'because God gave them that day as a day of freedom'.[5] Today there are no slaves in our society, but there exist forces of economic pressure which leave many of our people with little choice but to work on Sunday: the mega-store and supermarket and shopping arcade are the taskmasters of our time![6]

The observance of Sunday
Apart from participating in the Eucharist, how does a Christian fulfil the precept, 'Keep holy the Sabbath day'? Here we

consider some of the traditional spiritual works proposed for the Lord's Day.

We begin with a recommendation from a twelfth-century Irish homily. The author lists among the practices that are most suitable for Sunday: 'offering the Mass and prayer, the reading and writing of divinity, almsgiving to the poor and works of mercy in general'.[7] That final prescription regarding charitable works is interesting: it will recur again and again in subsequent writings. A homily in the Leabhar Breac enumerates three ways of refreshing the spirit on feastdays:
1) by preaching the word of God;
2) by offering the sacrifice;
3) by feeding and clothing the poor.[8]
Another homily of the period speaks of Sunday as 'a day for psalm-singing, celebration with preaching, the offering of the Mass, and feeding the poor'.[9] It is clear that Sunday, while being a day of rest, is by no means an idle or empty day. Apart from its liturgical and spiritual aspects, it has a definite social and charitable dimension.

Many centuries later this teaching is handed on in works of catechetical instruction. The Catechism of Andrew Donleavy, first published in 1742 in Irish and English, stresses the obligation to abstain from unnecessary servile work on Sunday, and then specifies the good works to be done on this day: 'To pray and do Godly works; such as to hear Mass punctually, to assist at the sermon, to read spiritual books, to say the beads, or do some other good works.'[10] In 1775 there appeared the first liturgical catechism to be published in Ireland. It bore the title, *A Practical Catechism on the Sundays, Feasts and Fasts of the Whole Year*, and was published by Richard Cross of Dublin. This catechism, with its inspiring section on Sunday, was sponsored by that remarkable churchman, John Carpenter, Archbishop of Dublin from 1770. Liturgical reform was central to his endeavours. He himself was imbued with the spirit of the liturgy and sought to share his vision with the people. Characteristically, he chose as his episcopal motto the liturgical acclamation 'Alleluia'.[11]

In Part 1, Section 1 of the catechism, we find the question: 'Why did God appoint a Sabbath?' The reply comes: 'in memory of creation and redemption'. More specifically it states: 'That man might not only give rest to his body but to his soul as well: by calling off his mind from the cares and pleasures of this life, to attend to higher and better things; namely, the consideration of the eternal Sabbath, or rest in the world to come, the avoiding of evil and the doing of good.'[12]

Carpenter's catechism presents a clear and simple theological vision of Sunday. It was chosen, we are told, 'in memory of our Saviour's Resurrection, and the coming down of the Holy Spirit; *these two mysteries being the accomplishment of our redemption*' (italics my own). The principle duties of this day include, in the first place, assisting at the holy sacrifice of the Mass with attention and devotion, and at the other public prayers in a spirit of adoration and thanksgiving. Then are listed among recommended Sunday observances:

1) 'attention to the word of God heard or read by us';
2) meditation: 'to enliven our faith and desires of that heavenly rest into which Christ entered by his Resurrection';
3) 'to improve the remainder of the day in doing good works, spiritual and corporal'.

Prayer and devotions

Even before the repeal of the penal laws, not only was the Mass being celebrated publicly but other forms of liturgical prayer and popular devotions were also made available to the Catholic community. In this section I draw my information mainly from the writings of Patrick Corish. Two of his books in particular shed light on the liturgical and devotional life of the Irish people. These are *The Irish Catholic Experience* and *The Catholic Community in the Seventeenth and Eighteenth Centuries*.

It is mainly in the towns that the development of afternoon and evening Sunday devotions took place. From the second decade of the eighteenth century the Franciscans and Dominicans gave a lead in popularising the devotion of exposition of the Blessed Sacrament on Sundays and holy days. It was something of a novelty in the Ireland of the time, and it seems that some of the diocesan clergy did not wholly approve of it. But a Jesuit writing from Dublin in 1747 exclaims with delight: 'We now begin to have Vespers sung and sermons preached in the afternoons. You see how peaceable times we enjoy.' From 1761 there are accounts of Sunday services at the Dominican church in Bridge street with Vespers and Rosary, followed by a sermon in the afternoon.[13]

During the first half of the nineteenth century, sodalities and confraternities multiplied in cities, especially in Dublin. For example, we hear of a Confraternity of the Blessed Sacrament which promoted all forms of eucharistic devotion, especially Benediction of the Blessed Sacrament. The Evening Office Society, founded by Peter Kenney in the 1790s, gathered its members each evening after work to recite Vespers and Compline in common. It is significant that here lay Catholics took the initiative. The Evening Office book, published in 1822, included daily Vespers and Compline in Latin and English.[14]

Sunday devotions were by no means confined to Dublin. In the middle of the eighteenth century, the Catholics of Wexford came in good numbers to celebrate Vespers with their clergy on Sunday evenings; they followed the service with their manuals of prayer.[15] Sung Vespers and Benediction were regular services in the towns of the diocese of Cloyne in 1775. As newly-appointed Archbishop of Armagh, Paul Cullen introduced novenas and Benediction to his archdiocese. In 1851 he initiated the Holy Week ceremonies. It seems that the people were delighted with the ceremonies. He in turn was deeply impressed by his people's devotion, but did not think much of their singing![16]

And so there is a tradition of other forms of liturgical celebration and popular devotions outside of Mass on Sunday afternoons and evenings. Not a strong tradition, perhaps, but still significant. In our time the Church, through the liturgical reforms of the Second Vatican Council, sought to revive

Vespers, the Evening Prayer of the Church, as a popular celebration in parishes. Somehow this has not really borne fruit in this country. Various factors can be adduced such as the introduction of Sunday evening Masses and a general decline in evening devotions.

Sunday with the emigrants

Irish emigrants brought with them to the four continents their love of the Mass and their fidelity to Sunday observance. A moving testimony to this is found in that gripping little book, *Rothar mór an tSaoil* (the great wheel of life), by Michael MacGowan, translated by Valentine Iremonger as, *The Hard Road to Klondike*.[17] It describes the day-to-day life of a group of Irishmen prospecting for gold in the bleak and rocky terrain of north-west Canada. Let us listen to the author's own words as he describes a Sunday in Klondike in those adventurous times:

> No matter where we were, we tried not to miss Mass if it was at all possible. We often walked ten miles for it, but I doubt if there was a priest within a hundred miles of where we were then. (He tells how that was changed with the arrival of a Fr Magee from Tyrone.)
> ... Even when we hadn't a priest living among us, we never liked to work on Sundays. When we couldn't hear Mass, a crowd of us would get together in one of the cabins and say the rosary – and say it heartfully. We weren't afraid of others listening to us. Many a time the cabin would be more than full for the rosary, and those who couldn't get in would go down on their knees outside; which often reminded me of home, for I frequently saw people kneeling outside the door of the church in Gortahork in the same way. (p.125)

Relaxation

Sunday is a feastday, 'the original feastday', according to the Liturgical Constitution of the Second Vatican Council. Now a feastday has a spiritual, familial and social dimension. This is conveyed by the Irish word, 'féile', which like *'fête'* or *'fiesta'*, implies a whole range of activities which supplement the liturgical celebration in church.

Sunday is a joyful day and one to be enjoyed. We may apply to it the words of Nehemiah: 'This day is holy to the Lord your God; do not mourn or weep. For this day is holy to our Lord; and do not be grieved, for the joy of the Lord is your strength.' (Ne 8:9) The idea of a Sabbath rest is positive and beautiful, but the attitude described as Sabbatarianism has little to commend it. It implies an over-strict interpretation of the Sunday rest, attributing to it all the restrictions of the Old Testament Sabbath, and even adding to them. We associate this perhaps with certain forms of Presbyterianism, but it has to be admitted that there is more than a streak of this in ancient Irish asceticism. The Cáin Domhnaigh or 'Law of Sunday', spoken of in the first chapter, is manifestly Sabbatarian in tone, and seems to have been influential in countries outside of Ireland. However, it is doubtful if this legislation was ever fully implemented. Moreover, in recent history, Irish Church policy has been on the whole moderate and tolerant with regard to the way people enjoy their Sunday.

I came across a small book called *Act for a Better Observation of the Lord's Day*, dated 1803. It expressly rules out the playing of hurling on Sunday. In mitigation of this apparently arbitrary ruling, it might be pointed out that this national game, up to the time that the rules were standardised and more powers conferred on the referee, could and did get out of hand. Be that as it may, the Catholic hierarchy did not support this prohibition of English law. Thomas William Croke (1832-1902), Archbishop of Cashel, was the first ecclesiastical patron of the Gaelic Athletic Association (GAA), and gave his active support to that organisation founded in 1844 to revive, support and popularise native Irish games. For Dr Croke mere idleness did not make for a better or holier Lord's Day. He recognised the real benefits accruing from physical, competitive games. He had no scruple about the playing of hurling or football, or any other game indeed, on Sunday. His only concern was that the players might be prevented from getting to Mass; and so he suggested that the best way to maintain Sunday observance (by which he meant attendance at Mass) was to arrange for parochial and other competitions on Sundays and holy days of obligation always to begin after two o'clock in the afternoon.[18]

What of other forms of relaxation? There was no prohibition on card playing, the holding of 'céilithe', attendance at plays, or other forms of entertainment. One traditional custom about which there were rather negative feelings on the part of the clergy was crossroads dancing. These dances, held on Sunday afternoons in parishes around the country, were very popular with the people, and have lasted down to modern times. The notion of crossroads dancing is sometimes parodied today by social commentators. For them it epitomises rural innocence in a repressed social order. The irony is that some of the clergy in the last century did not regard it as quite so innocent; in fact they viewed it as a threat to morals and so they expressly forbade it. A rather amusing incident is recounted by one Fr Patrick Kennedy, writing from Wexford in 1867. To avoid the attention of the parish priest, the local young people chose a remote site at the extreme edge of the parish to have their open-air dance. In fact it took place on a bridge separating two parishes. One can imagine the panic that ensued when, in the middle of their merrymaking, the dancing couples were surprised by the arrival of two angry parish priests converging on them from opposite sides of Ballymackessy bridge![19]

Concern of the pastors

In recent years Church leaders in Ireland have voiced their deep concern with the progressive secularisation of Sunday. More and more Sunday trading has become the norm with the result that, externally at least, there is little to distinguish the Christian Sabbath from other weekdays. This phenomenon manifested itself earlier in Britain where in 1985 the

Conservative government signalled its intention to abolish all remaining Sunday trading laws. Here in Ireland we quickly followed suit. Sunday trading on a large scale came about as a result of the enterprise of the business community. Our laws were slacker than in Britain, so the change of practice was introduced without government intervention.

In 1988 the Bishops of the Western Province issued a joint pastoral letter on Sunday Celebration. It treats of the nature of Sunday, day of the eucharistic assembly, day of rest, day of family and social solidarity. It takes issue with uncontrolled Sunday trading: 'We are strongly convinced that if Sunday were to become a full trading day it would have devastating effects on the day of the Lord.' While it appreciates the convenience that Sunday shopping represents for some shoppers, it reminds us that the primary concern for Christians must be the worthy celebration of the Lord's Day. It has this telling phrase: 'Sunday itself should not be traded at any price.'[20] The most recent and comprehensive treatment of the subject is to be found in the pastoral of Archbishop Dermot Clifford of Cashel and Emly, *The Meaning of Sunday* (Dublin: Messenger Publications, 1996). It deals with the liturgical, pastoral and social aspects of Sunday, as well as confronting the problem of Sunday trading.

It is not only Roman Catholic bishops who are concerned with this problem. In a joint statement issued in December 1995, the leaders of the four main Churches in Ireland (Catholic, Church of Ireland, Methodist and Presbyterian) spoke out on Sunday trading. They insisted that the Christian Sabbath must be maintained as 'a family day of rest, relaxation and corporate worship'. They point out the harmful social effects of the commercialisation of Sunday, and, on a point of justice, declare that 'the rights and welfare of shop workers must also be safeguarded'.[21]

In the light of Church teaching, the rest – in its spiritual, human and social aspects – is seen to provide the necessary ambience for the worship of God in the Eucharist as well as in other forms of public prayer and devotion. We need space and leisure, and the opportunity to take time off for God, for ourselves and for our families. The Christian Sunday is a multifaceted reality, and the Sabbath rest, properly understood, is a rich, attractive and challenging ideal. In *The Meaning of Sunday*, as well as in other pastoral writings of this kind, we are presented with a vision, both traditional and contemporary, of the Lord's Day which it behoves us to make our own. We must not lose the vision or shirk the challenge it presents us all with.

7
GatheRing the fRagments

After the miracle of the loaves and fish, Jesus told his disciples: 'Gather up what is left over, so that nothing is lost' (Jn 6: 12). Similarly, at the conclusion of our study of Sunday and Eucharist in Irish tradition, it now seems opportune to recapitulate a little and to draw what lessons we can from the centuries of Christian faith and devotion.

In the first chapter we observed the growing importance of Sunday in the ancient Irish Church. We learnt that as the Mother of Jesus holds first place among all women, so amongst the days of the week Sunday is the greatest. A day of remembrance, recalling all the *mirabilia Dei*, the wonderful works of God on behalf of his people, culminating in the paschal mystery of the Death, Resurrection and Glorification of Jesus. We could speak of a *sacrament of Sunday*, a sacred and effective sign of Christ's saving mysteries and of his abiding presence in the Church. Sunday is a sacramental day, recalling and reactivating the sacraments of Christian initiation; a blessed and venerable day which brings the people together in Church; a day of joy and exultation comparable to Easter. Finally, it is a day consecrated to the mystery of the Holy Trinity.

In the second chapter we attempted to reconstruct the Celtic Mass as it is known to us through the Stowe Missal and other liturgical documents. As the elaborate ceremonial unfolds, we get a sense of awe and mystery, with numerous unveilings and acts of reverence. At this stage of its development it had become to some extent romanised with the use of the Roman *canon missae*, but there are also elements borrowed from other liturgies both Western and Eastern. The Irish Church freely borrowed liturgical flowers from many gardens. But there are also features that are peculiarly Irish: thus the extended lists of biblical and native Irish saints which occur in the course of the Mass.

The Irish Church had a high regard for the word of God. It placed it on a par with the Eucharist itself. This is borne out in a Holy Thursday homily in the Leabhar Breac where it is explained that the Body of Christ is to be understood in three ways:

1) the body, born of the Virgin Mary (and rendered present in the sacrament);
2) Holy Church;
3) Holy Scripture.

It is this 'third body', Holy Scripture, that contemporary Irish Catholics need to read, hear, ponder and appreciate more and more. We need to acquire that 'warm and living love of Scripture', recommended by the Second Vatican Council. Here the liturgy can exercise its educational role in the prayers and ritual with which it surrounds the Gospel.

If the Book of Kells symbolises Ireland's veneration of the Scriptures, the Ardagh chalice proclaims its eucharistic faith and devotion. No material was too precious, no craftsmanship too perfect in the service of God's word and sacrament. The liturgies of word and sacrament are complementary: they are, according to Thomás à Kempis in his *Imitation of Christ*, the 'two tables set side by side in the storehouse of holy Church'. The 'book and the chalice' (*il libro e il calice*): these, according to Pope John XXIII, are the two most sacred objects placed before us in the celebration of the liturgy.

We noted a strong sense of the communion of Saints. This was expressed by the invocation of God's holy ones in the Mass. The 'world invisible' was a conscious presence, never so keenly felt as in the unfolding of the sacred mysteries. There was also a strong sense of Church and community. The elaborate and highly symbolic *fractio* (breaking of bread), witnessed to in some Celtic liturgies, manifested the unity of

Christ's body, the Church, and to the incorporation of all categories of people within it. The Eucharist was a true community celebration. There was no place for that narrow individualism which rates the value of the Mass in terms of personal satisfaction.

We noted how the Communion rite was characterised by a spirit of deep reverence combined with genuine joyfulness. Communion antiphons seem to have been especially popular and are a feature of all Celtic liturgies. They are scriptural in content and inviting in tone: 'Come and eat, take and drink.' This invitation is unrestricted and seems to imply that all received from the chalice. The reiterated alleluias, which conclude these verses, give a note of Easter joy to the celebration.

The great eucharistic hymn, *Sancti venite*, was part of the Communion rite, and may have been inspired by the earlier antiphons. Composed by an anonymous monk or cleric of the sixth century, it is the earliest eucharistic hymn of the Western Church, and can hold its own with the finest poems and sequences of the later medieval period. In chapter three we explored some of the riches of this composition which is a veritable treatise in poetic form on the mystery of the Eucharist. We admired its robust, joyful faith, its freshness and breadth of vision. It is truly universal in outlook: Christ died on behalf of all people, it proclaims, and all are invited to the Supper of the Lord. No more is required of those who approach the altar than that they do so with simple faith and eager longing. The '*Sancti venite*', it was suggested, is a hymn which, either in Latin or in the vernacular, merits a permanent place in the hymnody of the Irish Church.

In chapter four, 'From Age to Age', we saw how, in the course of time, a more rigorous approach to sacramental practice developed. A growing sense of personal unworthiness kept people from approaching the altar. As in other countries, the Irish faithful received the sacrament of Christ's body only at Easter and perhaps on a few other occasions in the year. And yet the teaching of such men as the twelfth century monk of

Roscrea, and later of Geoffrey Keating, was balanced and humane. What was important in their view was to have the right attitude and dispositions. Out of reverence one could abstain from receiving the King of Heaven, or, like Zacchaeus, gladly welcome the Lord under one's roof though conscious of personal sinfulness. The Church in every age must favour the *via media* in eucharistic practice. Today we readily and rightly respond to our Lord's invitation, 'Take and eat', and also – as communion from the chalice becomes more and more the norm – 'Take and drink'. That is certainly good and in conformity with early liturgical practice. What we must avoid, however, is a casual, indifferent attitude, one that is altogether at variance with New Testament teaching.

The Church's understanding of the eucharistic mystery has also evolved in the course of the centuries. Irish eucharistic faith and piety constantly centred on the doctrine of the real presence and on the memorial of the saving Passion and Death of Christ in the Mass. These will always remain constants in our teaching about the Mass while at the same time we venture to explore other aspects of the eucharistic mystery. The Eucharist, we observed, is a rich and multi-faceted reality, and today both priests and people can be enriched by new insights from contemporary sacramental theology.

The teaching of the Second Vatican Council endorsed many of these insights, and also sought to recover forgotten or neglected truths of earlier Christian tradition. As the great Jesuit scholar, J. A. Jungmann, once declared: in the household of the faith we must not be content to live in just one room where we feel comfortable, but rather freely explore the many other richly furnished apartments in our Father's house. The Mass is not only Real Presence and Sacrifice, and Christ is present not only in the consecrated bread and wine but also in the liturgical assembly and in the Word. As the late Mgr Seán Swayne so well put it, Mass-goers of our time need to be more conscious not only of Christ on the altar, but also of Christ *at and around* the altar.

A history of the Mass in Ireland remains to be written. But

in the course of the fourth chapter we traced in a general way the evolution of liturgical practice in this country throughout the centuries. The picture is not one of strict uniformity and unchanging tradition. After the disappearance of the Celtic rite there appeared other forms of liturgy, all Western and Roman in their main features: liturgies of the religious orders, Franciscan, Dominican, Norbertine and others. Then there were liturgies of English origin, notably the Sarum rite, incorporating the usages of Salsbury; I have heard that, to a lesser degree, the Winchester rite was also practised here. Then, following the Council of Trent, came the Missal of Pope St Pius V in 1570. This inaugurated the so-called Tridentine rite which remained in force up to our own times, but was replaced in 1970 by the Missal of Pope Paul VI which represents an enrichment as well as a thorough recasting of the previous Mass-book. This *Missale Romanum* itself is subject to further changes and revisions in accordance with liturgical requirements and pastoral needs. The liturgy, like the Church itself, is always in need of reform – *semper reformanda*. There is need too for inculturation, and it is gratifying to learn that the long-awaited new ICEL edition of the Roman Missal will incorporate in the main body of the work the feastdays of our national saints.

Fidelity to the Mass is certainly a strong feature of Irish Church history. This was never so clearly manifested as in the post-Reformation and Penal times. We must not over-idealise the situation however, or imagine that there were no abuses or defections. There were reprobate priests as well as lax and lazy layfolk in every age. Even the poet Raftery had to confess that as a young man he preferred to play cards and drink than to go to Mass on a Sunday ('B'fhearr liom go mór ag imirt 's ag ól ar maidin Domhnaigh ná ag triall chun an aifreann'). He bitterly reproached himself for this in his later poems. But in spite of inevitable defections, the overall picture is very impressive and shows great continuity. There were priests like Maurice McKenraghty and the Franciscan John Kearney who were truly martyrs of the Mass; and how many of our countrymen and women risked their lives to shelter such priests!

The tradition of a Mass-going people is well-established in the seventeenth and eighteenth centuries. The saying, 'it's the Mass that matters', certainly holds good for these and the following centuries. But we have no statistics to go on for these difficult times. When the first figures for religious practice appear in the 1830s, they are rudimentary and incomplete. They do reveal, however, that the level of attendance at Sunday Mass in rural areas – especially the Gaeltacht regions of the West – was much lower than what we might expect, between 25 per cent and 50 per cent. What some historians and sociologists have failed to take into account is that in these very poor areas the people often lacked even a rudimentary chapel and were probably obliged to travel long distances for their Sunday Mass. Those who gathered for worship at a Mass-rock or in a cabin were not subject to statistics and so were not included in the survey. This being said, however, it is true to add that in the second half of the nineteenth century there occurs a phenomenal increase in the numbers attending Mass throughout the country. This is due in great measure to the removal of the last vestiges of the Penal Laws, but also to the so-called 'Devotional revolution' inaugurated by Cardinal Paul Cullen. During his long period of pastoral ministry from 1849 to 1878, attendance at Sunday Mass increased rapidly, reaching almost the 100 per cent mark by the end of the century. This impressive achievement was sustained throughout the first half of this century, and indeed up to the mid 1960s, a decade which saw the beginning of profound social, economic and cultural change.

In recent decades the decline in religious practice is parallel with the decline in vocations to the priestly and religious life. In both cases the trend has been downward as in other European countries. However, non-attendance at Mass does not of itself signify loss of faith or abandonment of religion. A high proportion of young people, recently surveyed in the Limerick area, acknowledged that they prayed every day. But a faith that loses contact with the Eucharist may be seriously at risk if we take seriously Our Lord's words: 'unless you eat the flesh of the Son of man and drink his blood, you have no life in you' (Jn 6:52).

We have every reason to be concerned about falling numbers: Church leaders, and pastors generally, need to study the statistics carefully. At the same time, it may be suggested that mere head-counting is not what it's all about. Our concern should not simply be to fill our churches but also to ensure the quality of participation of those who attend. Is God glorified by full pews occupied by people with empty heads and hearts? Is mere physical presence enough if our places of worship are *spiritually* empty? The Law of Obligation may have worked in the past but is no longer effective. Nor is it desirable that people come to church because they feel obliged to do so out of fear of grave sin or through social convention or parental pressure. Rather, what is to be aimed at is an attitude of conviction, not coercion; what should motivate our people is not obligation but a need for, and love of, genuine *celebration*.

This leads us to a consideration of the Sunday Prayers of the People treated of in chapter five. Here, in these traditional 'paidreacha na ndaoine', we have a true and impressive spirituality of Sunday and the Sunday Mass. In these spontaneous compositions one can detect no sense of constraint, of a people reluctantly complying with Church law. On the contrary, they speak loudly and clearly of sincere faith and joyful expectation as the people of God makes its way to Mass. What motivated the faithful people was the anticipation of a joyful encounter, both at the individual and community levels, with their Lord and Saviour, Christ crucified and risen. 'Fáilte' is the word which keeps recurring: they welcomed Christ, King of Sunday, in word and sacrament, and above all at the moment of Communion.

We can learn not only from the prayers of the people but also from the way they worshipped and from the places in which they worshipped. In contrast with the large and impersonal buildings which provide the setting for Sunday Eucharist in so many of our towns and parishes today, the older tradition favoured a smaller spatial area, a house of God on a more human scale. This was true even in the Golden Age of Irish Christianity: one can cite the examples of Clonmacnois and Glendalough, monastic 'cities' in which there are a number of small or modest-sized churches rather than a single vast basilica or soaring cathedral. It was the Irish way to add on small churches or oratories, as the need arose, rather than to construct one mighty one.

During the Reformation era, and later in the penal times, there was little choice but to build modestly if at all. But our study of these centuries of repression is instructive, and can serve as an inspiration for our own times. It is not the building, however beautiful or grandiose, that constitutes the Church, but the assembly of God's people. St Augustine, addressing his people on the occasion of a church dedication, reminded them that it was they, not the temple of stone, who were the *ecclesia Dei*. Were our forebears who worshipped at Mass-rocks, in thatched cabins or in private homes, perhaps more conscious than we are of the fact that they constituted the *plebs Dei*, the people of God assembled for worship? Significantly, the place where they gathered for the Eucharist was called 'Teach an phobail' (the house of the people), and even today in Gaeltacht areas, the congregation is addressed as 'a phobal Dé' (people of God).

Again, the tradition of the House Mass or Station Mass has something to teach us at a time when people complain about the size and impersonality of our church buildings. In the Ireland of the post-famine times up to the beginning of this century, the liturgy had a firm base in the home as well as in the local church. Baptisms, marriages and wakes took place in the home, as well as the occasional Station Mass – the latter especially in preparation for Christmas and Easter. (There is an interesting parallel here with Jewish custom whereby the liturgy is both synagogue-based and home-based.) All that has survived – rescued by the post-conciliar reforms – is the House Mass. This invites some reflections.

It seems to me that there are two important values

associated with the House Mass or small group Mass. The first is that it *brings God into the home*; it helps make the Christian household a place of prayer and family worship. In so many homes today there are no religious objects of any kind to be seen, and family prayer is a thing of the past. An occasional celebration of the Eucharist, carefully prepared and carried out with full participation of the family group, would surely nurture the seeds of faith that may lie dormant in the minds and hearts of family members.

Another value of the House Mass is that it acts as a bridge between home and Church. The experience of intimacy, sharing and interiority, which we associate with the small-group liturgy, can lead to a real understanding and appreciation of the mystery of the Eucharist in a more communal setting. Once faith is awakened, and we begin to recognise the Lord in the 'breaking of bread', then every Mass is perceived and valued as an epiphany of the Risen Lord. The family or small group cannot remain sufficient unto itself. Each one must have the courage and generosity to join in worship with the full assembly of God's people. The parish or community Mass, whatever its shortcomings at the liturgical level, draws together the Christian assembly, the *ecclesia Dei*, in all its diversity. Here at Sunday Mass is Christ in our midst, our Shepherd and King, teaching, healing, nourishing, leading us in his worship of the Father. Here too the Spirit is at work, making of all who share in the one bread and one cup 'one body, one spirit, in Christ'.

In the penultimate chapter we considered the Sunday rest in all its aspects. Far from being negative and restrictive, the Sunday rest is positive and liberating. It is necessary both at the human and spiritual level. We need time off for ourselves, for our families and for God. Sunday is a day of worship, it is a festive day which reqires an ambience of relaxation and quiet. There must be at least one day in the week free from the pressure of work, study and other constraints.

Here we confronted the problem of Sunday trading which, in the unlimited and unregulated form it has assumed in recent years, poses a serious threat to the Christian Sabbath. Supermarket companies, vying with one another for a monopoly of trade, insist on opening their premises practically on all Sundays of the year. How long, one wonders, can Easter remain an exception? Church leaders have spoken out against the abuse of Sunday trading, and even the trade unions have had to intervene to protect the rights of their members.

The Church cannot compel people to refrain from working on Sundays any more than it can compel them to attend Mass. What it can and *must* do is to campaign for its sacred days and seasons which are being increasingly secularised and trivialised. It must encourage its members to opt willingly and joyfully for the full observance of Sunday as a day of rest, of corporate worship, of family cohesion, of acts of kindness, as well as a day of relaxation, play and creative leisure. Not just a 'funday', nor a dour day either! There is need for a strong, ongoing catechesis of Sunday and the Sunday Eucharist, a *Catechesis Celtica* for our times and culture.

The Eucharist has been described as the heartbeat of the Church's life. It is indeed central to the celebration of the Lord's Day; and yet, important as the Mass is, it does not constitute the sum-total of Sunday observance. At the personal and community levels, there are other ways of sanctifying this day which it may be well for us to recall at this stage.

Among the hallowed practices associated with Sunday are personal prayer and meditation. Some form of spiritual reading (*lectio divina*) is appropriate and highly recommended. Lay Catholics, and perhaps we priests and religious as well, need to become more familiar with the inspired scriptures. It has been observed by more than one commentator that one of the great lacks of the contemporary Irish Church is a deep and strong biblical culture. How much more would people derive from the Mass if they familiarised themselves with the sacred texts and made them the object of their prayer and meditation?

Among the religious practices associated with Sunday is the recalling of Baptism. This can be made part of the opening section of Sunday Mass with the blessing and sprinkling of the assembly with holy water. At a personal level, parishioners may wish to renew their baptismal promises, and this could be done at the baptismal font which is the 'Sunday's Well' or 'Tobar Rí an Domhnaigh' of each parish. Another more universally practised custom is the visiting of the cemeteries on Sunday. This is a genuine act of *pietas*, one that corresponds with a deeply human and Christian instinct. In Irish tradition the grave or tomb is the 'place of resurrection', and what better day to visit our departed loved ones than that day which celebrates the Resurrection itself. In many parishes it is the custom on the Sundays of November to have the Rosary recited publicly in the parish cemeteries.

Sunday is incomplete without its 'liturgical crown', Vespers, the Evening Prayer of the Church. The Liturgy Constitution of the Second Vatican Council and the General Instruction on the Liturgy of the Hours strongly recommend that the chief hours, especially Vespers, be celebrated in church on Sundays and the more solemn feasts. The idea is by no means alien to the Irish Church, for we have seen how in the eighteenth century, even before the repeal of the Penal Laws, afternoon and evening devotions, including Vespers and Benediction, were regular features of Catholic devotional practice, especially in large urban areas. Can this idea be revived and given actuality in the very different society of our day?

With the multiplication of Sunday Masses, as well as with the reduction in numbers of clergy, the notion of parochial Vespers on Sunday evening may seem Utopian. Evening devotions have long been in decline. But we must not look only at the difficulties but also at the possibilities. I discussed some of these possibilities in my previous book, *Welcome to Sunday* (chapter 8, 'Evening Prayer, Evening Devotions'). I suggested that an adapted form of liturgical Evening Prayer could be organised by lay groups within the parish. I also believe that religious communities, especially monastic communities, could do even more to facilitate lay participation in the Liturgy of the Hours. Monastic liturgy differs in several respects from that of the parishes, but it too is the prayer and worship of the Church, the whole People of God. Traditionally, monastic communities warmly welcome visitors to their liturgy, and that includes in a special way the celebration of the Eucharist and of Vespers on Sundays and solemnities.

And so let us restore to the Lord's Day its liturgical crown, and thus make Sunday truly a 'day and a night for answering Christ'. Liturgical Evening Prayer nicely rounds off the worship of this day, extending the prayer and thanksgiving of the Eucharist to the closing hours. Of its nature neither clerical nor monastic, it invites the presence of the people of God without restriction, and that includes the parish community. It is a prayerful office, offering our people a taste of that contemplative dimension of the liturgy sometimes lacking in the rather hurried assemblies of Sunday morning. For those who take part, of whatever age group, this can be a revelation of what Sunday could and should be: a celebration, prayerful, praiseful and joyful, of the paschal mystery of the Death and Resurrection of Jesus in which we share through Baptism and Eucharist. It proclaims the good news of the Gospel and leads us to exclaim: 'This is the day which the Lord has made, let us rejoice and be glad.'

notes

Chapter 1: The Shaping of Sunday

1. Sun worship was very strong among the Celts. The sun and fire gods were the highest among their divinities. In such a religious climate the appelation Sunday, *dies solis*, could well be considered inappropriate for Christians. On the other hand, the Christian symbolism of the sun was well known to the Irish Church. This is witnessed to in early Irish prayers where we meet such expressions as 'True light that enlightens every darkness', 'We believe and adore the true Sun, Christ', and 'King of the blazing sun'.

2. See P. W. Joyce, *Irish Names of Places*, vol. 1 (Gill & Son, Dublin, 1910), pp. 318-20.

3. *The Mass of the Roman Rite*, vol. 1 (Benziger, New York, 1951), pp. 171-2.

4. See Leslie Hardinge, *The Celtic Church in Britain* (SPCK, London, 1972) chapter 3, 'The Christian Year', especially pp. 75-90.

5. The full reference to this book by Rordorf is: *Sunday, The History of the Day of Rest in the Earliest Centuries of the Christian Church* (SCM Press, London, 1968). This quotation is from p. 146. See also pp. 118-53.

6. Hardinge, work cited, pp. 77-8.

7. Hardinge, p. 78, and Rordorf, *Sunday*, p. 153.

8. From Adomnán's *Life of Columba*, edited by A. Orr Anderson and M. Ogilvie Anderson (London, Nelson, 1961), p. 523.

9. See Peter O'Dwyer, *Céil Dé, Spiritual Reform in Ireland, 750-900* (Taillura, Dublin, 1981), pp. 116-21.

10. Published by T. & T. Clark, Edinburgh, 1989. See pp. 50-54.

11. See Michael Maher, 'Sunday in the Irish Church', in *The Irish Theological Quarterly*, 1994: 3, p. 163.

12. 'The Significance of Sunday: Three Ninth-Century Catecheses', in *Worship*, vol. 64, no. 6, (November 1990),

pp. 533-44. *Worship* is published by the Monks of St John's Abbey, Collegeville, Minnesota 56321, USA.

13. O'Loughlin, work cited, p. 536.
14. This idea is developed by Fr O'Loughlin, p. 541, following Robert Taft SJ.
15. See Michael Curran, *The Antiphonary of Bangor and the Early Irish Monastic Liturgy* (Irish Academic Press, Dublin, 1984).
16. Curran, work cited, p. 186.
17. Text in F.E. Warren, *The Antiphonary of Bangor* (Henry Bradshaw Society, London, 1893), HBS 4 and 10. The hymn is also given in *The Celtic Saints* by D. Pochin Mould (Clonmore and Reynolds, Dublin, 1956), p. 150. For a detailed commentary, see Michael Curran, work cited, pp. 66-73.
18. *Pastoral Liturgy* (Challoner, London, 1962). Chapter 5, 'Fides Trinitatis', pp. 32-7. Above quote, p. 35.
19. 'Irish Prayer in the Early Middle Ages'. Translated from the German by Patrick Rogers CP in *Milltown Studies*, no. 9, 1982, p. 32.

Chapter 2: The Mass in Ancient Ireland

1. In preparing this chapter I have consulted the following: F. Warren, *The Liturgy and Ritual of the Celtic Church* (Clarendon Press, Oxford, 1881); H. Jenner, 'Celtic Rite', in *The Catholic Encyclopedia*, Tome 3, pp. 493-504; John Ryan, 'The Mass in the Early Irish Church', in *Studies* (Winter 1961), pp. 371-84; W. Godel, 'Irish Prayer in the Early Middle Ages', in *Milltown Studies* (Autumn 1979), pp. 60-99; D. Pochin Mould, 'The Mass and the Liturgy', in *The Celtic Saints, Our Heritage* (Clonmore and Reynolds, Dublin, 1956), pp. 56-68; D. Ó Laoghaire, 'The Eucharist in Irish Spirituality', in *Doctrine and Life* (December 1982), pp. 595-607; F. O'Briain, 'The Blessed Eucharist in Irish Liturgy and Spirituality', in the symposium *Studia Eucharistica* (Antwerp, 1946), pp. 216-45; P. Ní Chatháin, in, 'The Liturgical Background of the

Derrynaflan Altar Service', in *Journal of the Royal Society of Antiquaries of Ireland*, vol. 110 (1980), pp. 127-48.2.

2. E. Cullinan, 'The History of the Liturgy in Ireland', in *New Liturgy*, no. 66 (Autumn 1989), pp. 17-21.

3. A. Martimort, *The Church at Prayer, The Eucharist* (Irish Univ. Press, 1973), p. 31.

4. 'The Mass in the Early Irish Church', in *Studies*, vol. 50 (Winter 1961), pp. 371-84.

5. Due to a misplacing of the pages in the bound manuscript, this and other preliminary items are incorrectly found in the Canon of the Mass.

6. See Françoise Henry, *The Book of Kells* (Thames & Hudson, London, 1974), pp. 151 and 153.

7. *The Celtic Saints*, p. 56.

8. 'The Mass in the Early Irish Church', pp. 379-80. Work cited in note 1 above.

9. J. Hennig, 'Old Ireland and her Liturgy', in *Old Ireland*, edited by R. McNally (Gill & Son, Dublin, 1965), pp. 60-84.

10. Here I follow Patrick O'Reilly, 'The Fractio Panis in the Stowe Missal', in *Iris Hibernia*, vol. 4, no. 1, 1958, pp. 62-8.

11. D. Ó Laoghaire, 'The Eucharist in Irish Spirituality', p. 597, work cited in note 1 above.

12. Quoted by W. Godel, 'Irish Prayer in the Early Middle Ages', p. 75. Work cited in note 1 above.

13. Quoted by D. Ó Laoghaire, work cited, p. 600.

14. Here I follow, with slight adaptations, Fr John Ryan's translation in the article already cited.

Chapter 3: *'Sancti venite'*, an Ancient Eucharistic Hymn

1. The beautiful melody to accompany the Latin hymn was composed by Fr Edward (Eddie) Jones, an Irish Redemtorist from Dundalk, Co. Louth. The hymn with its music was published in 1930 in the *Redemptorist Record*. Fr Jones, who was organist and choir-master in Dundalk, died in 1963. The Latin text with musical notation and

English translation is to be found in *The Music of What Happens* by John Ó Riordáin (Columba Press, Dublin, 1996), p. 82.

2. See his book, *The Antiphonary of Bangor and the Early Irish Monastic Liturgy* (Irish Academic Press, 1984), pp. 47-9.

3. See 'The Blessed Eucharist in Irish Liturgy and History', in *Studia Eucharistica* (Antwerp, 1946), pp. 216-45.

4. *La Dévotion à l'Eucharistie* (Gembloux, 1946), pp. 39-41.

5. Quoted by F. O'Briain, work cited, p. 221.

6. See 'Old Ireland and her Liturgy', in *Old Ireland* (Gill & Son, Dublin, 1965), p. 78.

7. Dr Pochin Mould has availed of the English prose rendering given in *The Antiphonary of Bangor* (Henry Bradshaw Society, London, 1893), 2 vols.

8. See the Stowe Missal, Warren (ed.), in *The Liturgy and Ritual of the Celtic Church*, (Clarendon Press, Oxford, 1881) p. 242.

9. Quoted in my article, 'Holy Things for the Holy', in *Hallel*, vol. 14, no. 2, pp. 175-80.

10. See O'Briain, work cited, p. 225.

11. Quoted by D. Ó Laoghaire in 'The Eucharist and Irish Spirituality', in *Doctrine and Life* (December 1982), vol. 32, no.10 p. 596. A full translation of the hymn is given in *The Glenstal Bible Missal* for the feast of St Patrick.

12. *The Antiphonary of Bangor and the Early Irish Monastic Liturgy* (Irish Academic Press, Dublin, 1984) p. 48.

13. Work cited, p. 49.

14. Work cited, p. 49.

Chapter 4: From Age to Age

1. See Michael Maher, 'Sunday in the Irish Church', in *The Irish Theological Quarterly*, vol. 60, (1994), no. 3, p. 169.

2. See Archdale King, *Liturgies of the Past* (Longman, London, 1959), pp. 280-326.

3. Here we follow W. Hawkes, 'The Liturgy in Dublin, 1200-1500', in *Reportorium Novum*, vol. 2, no. 1 (1957-8), pp. 33-67.

4. W. Hawkes, work cited, p. 39.
5. *The Stripping of the Altars* (Yale University Press, 1992), pp. 29-31. An example of an Easter sepulchre in Ireland is to be found at Kinsale in the pre-Reformation church of St Multose.
6. See W. Godel, 'Irish Prayer in the Early Middle Ages (1)', in *Milltown Studies*, no. 4, (1979), pp. 63-4. Also J. Ryan, 'The Mass in the Early Irish Church', in *Studies*, (Winter 1961), pp. 372, 373 and 383.
7. Quoted by D. Ó Laoghaire in 'The Eucharist in Irish Spirituality', in *Doctrine and Life* (December 1982), p. 607.
8. Quoted by Ó Laoghaire, work cited, pp. 599-600.
9. See Gerard Murphy, 'Eleventh or Twelfth Century Irish Doctrine Concerning the Real Presence', in *Medieval Studies* – Presented to Aubrey Gwynn SJ. Edited by J. Watt, J. Morrall and F. Martin. (Printed by Colm O'Lochlainn at The Three Candles, Fleet Street, Dublin, 1961), pp. 19-28.
10. G. Murphy, work cited, p. 21.
11. Gill & Macmillian, Dublin, 1985, pp. 55-7. See also M. Maher in article cited in note 1 above.
12. Work cited, p. 75 ff.
13. Cotter, work cited, pp. 100-101.
14. Work cited, pp. 56-7.
15. Work cited, pp. 93-6 and 127.
16. Quotation from article by G. Murphy, cited in note 9 above. See p. 27.
17. From MS 667 in the library of Trinity College, Dublin. The reference was supplied to me by my colleague, Br Colmán Ó Clabaigh.
18. Cf. M. Maher in article cited note above, p. 174.
19. See A. King, work cited note 2 above, p. 291.
20. 'The History of the Liturgy in Ireland', in *New Liturgy*, no. 66, 1990, pp.17-21.
21. Columba Press, Dublin, 1996.
22. Work cited, p.8.

23. Quoted by Antonia Fraser in *Cromwell, Our Chief of Men* (London 1973), p. 347.
24. Good up-to-date biographies include *Oliver Plunkett in his own Words* by Desmond Forristal (Veritas, Dublin, 1975), and *Oliver Plunkett, New Saint*, by Tomás Ó Fiaich (Veritas, Dublin, 1975).
25. This and some other information I have gleaned from *Some Irish Heroes of the Mass* by Father Augustine OFM Cap (Dublin, 1945).
26. Quoted by M. Maher in article cited note 1 above, p. 176.
27. *The Irish Catholic Experience*, p. 133.
28. Corish, work cited, pp. 128-30. For a very thorough study of the subject, *confer:* 'Mass Rocks' by Margaret Kelly, in *Souvenir Catalogue for the Third Tóstal Display*, Section 1, Part 38 (St Patrick's College, Maynooth, 1955).
29. 'The Eucharist in Irish Spirituality', work cited, pp. 603-4.
30. *The Irish Catholic Experience*, pp. 166-7.
31. 'The Eucharist in Irish Spirituality', work cited, p. 602.
32. See Maher, work cited, p. 178.
33. See 'The Station Mass' in *The Small-Group Mass* (Dublin Diocesan Liturgical Commission, *circa* 1970). The subject also treated of by J. Cunnane, 'The Neighbourhood Mass', in *The Furrow*, vol. 19, 1968, pp. 559-70.
34. Quoted by J. B. O'Connell in his English edition of *Liturgical Renewal* by Josef Jungmann SJ (Burns & Oates, London, 1965), p. 43.

Chapter 5: Sunday Prayers of the People
1. Douglas Hyde's *The Religious Songs of Connacht*, first published in 1906, was re-issued in 1972 by Irish University Press. Ní Ógáin's *Dánta Dé* was published in Dublin in 1928. *Ár bPaidreacha Dúchais* was published by FÁS, Dublin, in 1975, and Redmond's *Prayers of Two Peoples* by Veritas Publications, Dublin, 1996.
2. Cf. B. Fischer, 'Begrüssung des Sonntags', in *Der Sonntag*, edited by A. Alternatt and Th. Schnitker (Würzburg, 1986), pp. 290-98. See also my article,

'Jewish Sabbath, Christian Sunday', in *Doctrine and Life* (November 1982).

3. Here I follow a line of thought well expounded by Fr Diarmuid Ó Laoghaire in his writings. Fr John Ó Ríordáin suggests the connection between the idea of *Kurios* and *Rí* in *Irish Catholics* (Veritas, Dublin, 1980), pp. 53-4.
4. From notes compiled by Fr Diarmuid Ó Laoghaire and made available to me with other material by Annraoi Ó Braonáin of Dublin.
5. *The Furrow* (June 1992), pp. 372-3.
6. *Ár bPaidreacha Dúchais*, no. 77, p. 32.
7. Ibid., no. 89, p. 36.
8. Ibid., no. 123, p. 44. This seems to echo a line in the Anima Christi Prayer: '*Ne permittas me separari a te*', 'Do not allow me to be separated from you'.
9. Ibid., no. 136. The rough translation is my own.
10. Quoted by D. Ó Laoghaire, 'The Celtic Monk at Prayer', in *Monastic Studies* 13 (1983), p. 129.
11. *Prayers of Two Peoples*, no. 21, p. 33.
12. *Ár bPaidreacha Dúchais* no. 120, p. 43; translation my own.
13. Work cited note 3, p. 37. It is interesting that already in the late medieval period the expression 'King of the Sunday' was known as a form of address to Christ.

Chapter 6: At Prayer and at Play

1. Quoted by Thomas O'Loughlin in his article, 'The Significance of Sunday: Three Ninth-Century Catecheses' in *Worship*, vol. 64, no. 6 (November 1990), p. 538.
2. Cf. M. Maher, 'Sunday in the Irish Church', in *The Irish Theological Quarterly*, vol. 60, no. 3, p. 165.
3. Subtitle, *A Liberties Childhood* (Brandon Books, Kerry), Chapter 9, 'Sunday', pp. 126-44.
4. Cf. C. Williams, 'Work and Rest', in *Doctrine and Life*, (September 1969), pp. 503-8. I have dealt with the human and spiritual aspects of the Sunday rest in *Welcome to Sunday* (Veritas, Dublin, 1980), pp. 45-56.

5. Cf. *Irish Biblical Apocrypha*, ed. M. Herbert & M. McNamara (Edinburgh, 1989), p. 51.
6. At the time of writing, the Irish Trade Union Movement has asserted the rights of its members to observe Sunday as a non-working day. Interestingly, the early French socialist, Pierre Proudhon, declared that Sunday was 'the one day in the week when servants regained the dignity of human beings and stood again on a level with their masters'. (Quoted by Archbishop Clifford in *The Meaning of Sunday*.)
7. Cf. M. Maher, 'Sunday in the Irish Church', work cited in note 2 above, p. 166.
8. M. Maher (ed.), *Irish Spirituality* (Columba Press, Dublin, 1981), p. 44. Cf. also J. Ó Ríordáin, *The Music of What Happens* (Columba Press, Dublin, 1996), pp. 76-8.
9. M. Maher, *Irish Spirituality*, pp. 44-5.
10. Cf. M. Maher, 'Sunday in the Irish Church', pp. 176-7. This catechism, first published in Paris, ran into several editions. I have consulted the third edition, published by Duffy's of Dublin in 1858.
11. Cf. Tomás de Bhál, 'Irish Liturgical Resurgence in the 18th Century', in *New Liturgy*, no. 28 (Winter 1980-81), pp. 2-7.
12. A copy of this catechism forms part of the de Bhál collection in St Patrick's College, Carlow.
13. Patrick Corish, *The Catholic Community*, p. 85.
14. Corish, *The Irish Catholic Experience*, p. 170.
15. Ibid., p. 133.
16. Ibid., p. 188.
17. Published by Rontledge and Kegan Paul, London, 1973.
18. Cf. M. Tierney, *Croke of Cashel* (Gill & Macmillan, Dublin, 1976), pp. 189-204, 'The Gaelic Athletic Association'.
19. Corish, *The Irish Catholic Experience*, pp. 176-7.
20. Published in *Intercom* (June 1988), p. 8.
21. Published in *Doctrine and Life* (December 1995), p. 697.

BIBLIOGRAphy

Clifford, Archbishop Dermot, *The Meaning of Sunday*. A pastoral message by the Archbishop of Cashel and Emly (Messenger Publications, Dublin, 1996).

Corish, Patrick, *The Irish Catholic Experience* (Gill & Macmillan, Dublin, 1985); and *The Catholic Community in the 17th and 18th Centuries* (Helicon History of Ireland series; Helicon Ltd, Dublin, 1981).

Cullinan, Edmond, 'The History of the Liturgy in Ireland', in *New Liturgy*, no. 66, autumn 1990, pp. 17-21.

De Bhál, Tomás, 'Patterns of Prayer and Devotion, 1750-1850', in *Studies in Pastoral Liturgy*, vol. 3, edited by Placid Murray (The Furrow Trust and Gill & Son, Dublin, 1967).

Dublin Diocesan Liturgical Commission, *Celebrating Sunday – Mass on the Evening before Sundays and Holydays*. A pamphlet (Veritas, Dublin, 1983).

Hyde, Douglas, *The Religious Songs of Connacht* (Irish University Press, 1972 a reprint from the 1906 edition).

Maher, Michael (ed.), *Irish Spirituality* (Veritas, Dublin, 1981); and 'Sunday in the Irish Church', in *The Irish Theological Quarterly*, 1994, no.3, vol. 60, pp. 161-84.

Moloney, Bernard, 'The Vigil Mass', in *Intercom* (July 1988).

Ó Laoghaire, Diarmuid, *Our Mass, Our Life*, short booklet on Irish traditions and prayers. (Irish Messenger Publications, Dublin, 1968). *Ár bPaidreacha Dúchais*, traditional Irish folk-prayers, many of them relating to Sunday and the Mass (FÁS,

Dublin, 1975). Also 'The Eucharist in Irish Spirituality', in *Doctrine and Life* (December 1982), pp. 595-607.

O'Loughlin, Thomas, 'The Significance of Sunday: three Ninth-Century Catecheses' in *Worship* (November 1990).

Ó Ríordáin, John, *Irish Catholics – Tradition and Transition.* (Veritas, Dublin, 1980); and *The Music of What Happens*, a book about Celtic spirituality including the Mass in Ireland (Columba Press, Dublin, 1996).

Redmond, Stephen, *Prayers of Two Peoples*, traditional Irish and Scottish verse-prayers (Veritas, Dublin, 1996).

Ryan, Vincent, *Welcome to Sunday* (Dublin, Veritas, 1980) Also 'Planning Sunday', in *Intercom* (April 1981); 'Jewish Sabbath, Christian Sunday', in *Doctrine and Life* (November 1982), pp. 533-40.